THRIVING TEAMS

THRIVING TEAMS

When Teams Unite, Align and Achieve

CLAIRE GRAY

Dedication

To my One Team – Ben, Jackson and Harvey xo

Acknowledgment of Country

I acknowledge the Arakwal people of the Bundjalung Nation, the Traditional Custodians of the land on which this book was written. I pay my respects to Elders past, present and emerging.

Contents

PART 1
PURPOSE

PART 2
RELATIONSHIPS

PART 3
ACCOUNTABILITY

PART 4
CONNECTION

PART 5
CHALLENGE AND SUPPORT

PART 6
ALIGNMENT

About the Author

Claire Gray is passionate about building high-performing teams and leaders so they can thrive. With over 20 years working in leadership and team performance, Claire has partnered with fast-growing scale-ups, and established corporates, government, and not-for-profits—across Australia, New Zealand, Asia, and the UK.

What ties it all together is her ability to cut through the noise, get to the heart of what's really going on in a team, and help leaders turn that into lasting results.

As the founder of Thriving Culture, Claire works with CEOs and leadership teams to strengthen capability, embed purpose-led cultures, and create environments where people genuinely want to do their best work. She runs successful leadership development programs and speaks at conferences and events.

She is the author of *Thriving Leaders: Learn the Skills to Lead Confidently* and the host of the *Thriving Leaders Podcast*, where she interviews global thought leaders. Interviewees have included Amy Edmondson, David Clutterbuck, and Dermot Crowley—all of whom feature in this book.

Claire holds a Master of Business (Human Resource Management), a Bachelor of Behavioural Science, and advanced accreditations in executive and team coaching. She studied *The Art and*

Practice of Leadership Development at Harvard Kennedy School, is a Professional Certified Coach with the International Coaching Federation, a certified Facet5 practitioner, and a graduate of the Global Team Coaching Institute.

Based in Byron Bay, Claire balances her work and family life, with her husband and two boys. You'll often find her on a lighthouse walk or at the beach. She loves travelling and going to the gym, and enjoys a hit of tennis.

Acknowledgements

It really does take a team to write a book. See what I did there!

A huge thank you to Amy Edmondson for writing the foreword and to David Clutterbuck for writing the afterword. I honestly couldn't think of two better people to bookend *Thriving Teams*. They are both leaders I deeply admire, and their thought leadership and research are foundations I draw on every day in my own work.

To the standout case study interviews: Jeremy Summers (Insync), Matt Carroll (Australian Olympic Committee), Joanna Green and Melissa Lyon (Hive Legal), and Greg Pickering (Australian Financial Complaints Authority). Thank you for your time, energy, and for so openly sharing your stories. Your experiences brought this book to life.

To the eight thought leaders who joined me on the *Thriving Leaders Podcast* and generously shared their insights: Amy Edmondson, David Clutterbuck, Dermot Crowley, Claire De Carteret, Kaye-Monk Morgan, Grant Gemmell, Justin Williams, and Leo Bottary. I am grateful for your wisdom and the generosity with which you contributed to these pages.

To my amazing clients—you inspire and motivate me. I learn so much from every engagement with you, and your challenges, insights, and wins have added to the richness of what's captured in these pages. Thank you for trusting me and your teams to partner together.

To the talented crew who helped bring this book to life: Erin O'Dwyer from Good Prose Studio for your editing brilliance; Lara Evans from Little L Designs for designing another epic cover; Michael Hanrahan and the team at Publish Central for guiding the publishing process; Anita Saunders for your sharp proofreading eye; and Tiffany Richmond for recording the audiobook so beautifully.

Behind the scenes, this book wouldn't have come together without my team. Ben Gray, who patiently read the entire manuscript and gave me the kind of feedback only a partner can give. Jo Lumanog—my secret weapon—for checking every detail, compiling references, designing the models, and the mammoth task of editing the audiobook. Megan Dela Cruz for listening to the audiobook, reading line by line to make sure it was perfect.

To those who helped me find the right stories or who were a sounding board along the way—Amie Wallis, Adrienne Trumbull, Clare Slade, James Garriock, Erika Szerda, Mark Hoppe, Dimi Patitsas and Jodi Geddes—thank you.

And finally, to my family—Ben, Jackson, and Harvey. You are my One Team. This book wouldn't exist without your love, humour, and unwavering support. One day you'll admit that I am funny. But now that it's in print, it's official: I am funny!

Foreword

I am delighted to introduce *Thriving Teams*. Claire Gray has written a book that is both timely and timeless: timely because today's organisations face unprecedented complexity and change, and timeless because the essence of teamwork—people coming together to achieve what none could do alone—will always remain essential.

We live in an era of heightened ambiguity. Hybrid work, economic pressures, and technology disruption make the act of leading and working in teams harder than ever. In such an environment, thriving takes work. Too often, teams stagnate in complacency or fracture into dysfunction. Yet as Claire argues—and demonstrates with practical tools—teams can move beyond simply performing. They can truly thrive.

One of the central insights of this book is the role of accountability. For too many, accountability has become synonymous with blame. But Claire sees it differently: accountability is a privilege. It is the opportunity to own your contribution, to shape outcomes, and to exercise judgment and responsibility. To be given accountability is to be trusted. This is entirely consistent with how I have defined accountability in my work—as psychological ownership of results. It's an internal commitment to do everything you can to uphold standards and to contribute to achieving a team's goals. Claire's book shows how accountability can ripple through organisations:

from individual ownership, to mutual commitments within teams, to collective responsibility across stakeholders. This systemic ripple shapes cultures where people step up—not out of fear of blame, but out of pride and purpose.

Another key theme is the art of high-quality conversation, a topic she and I discussed on the *Thriving Leaders Podcast*. Teams succeed or fail based on the quality of their dialogue. Yet most of us have been tacitly trained in impression management—looking good—and remain under-trained in the skills of candid, constructive debate. Claire introduces practical frameworks, including her healthy debate model, to equip leaders and teams to move past either polite avoidance or destructive conflict. High-quality conversations are rare, but when they occur, they create clarity, alignment, and progress. As I often tell leaders, psychological safety is not the end goal; it is the enabler of rigorous, forward-moving dialogue directed at achieving a team's real goals. *Thriving Teams* gives leaders concrete ways to build that capability.

Perhaps most importantly, this book underscores a truth I deeply believe: thriving teams are learning teams. In today's uncertain world, learning together—through curiosity, feedback, experimentation, and reflection—is not optional. It is the only way teams adapt and innovate. Claire brings this to life with stories, tools, and exercises that help teams normalise mistakes, celebrate intelligent failures, and grow stronger together. Claire even recounts a near-miss during the recording of the *Thriving Leaders Podcast* interview with me. I wasn't aware of this until I read the manuscript, but she uses it as a vivid example of how mistakes and failures can become opportunities for learning.

Claire has written a book that is practical, relevant, and accessible. It offers a model for diagnosing where your team stands, language for the often-messy conversations teams need to have, and tools to strengthen purpose, connection, and alignment. But more than that, it invites leaders and teams to take responsibility for their shared future. This is not a book to read passively; it is a book to work with, to return to, and to use as a catalyst for real change.

If you are a leader wondering how to unite your team, how to strengthen accountability without blame, how to cultivate debate without division, or how to keep learning in a world of constant change—this book is for you. And if you are a team member eager to contribute more fully, to engage in healthier dialogue, and to grow alongside your colleagues, this book is also for you.

I encourage you to lean in, reflect, and, most importantly, to put these ideas into practice. The rewards—greater trust, stronger performance, and a sense of genuine thriving—are well worth the effort.

Amy C. Edmondson
Cambridge, Massachusetts
USA

Introduction

The whole is greater than the sum of its parts.

— Aristotle

Why I wrote this book

I have always been fascinated by people—how they behave, what makes them tick, and how they interact with others. The dynamics between people led me to study a Bachelor of Behavioural Science. The dynamics within teams shift from one-to-one relationships to group norms that are created. These influences shape individual behaviours, which in turn affect the outcomes that teams can achieve.

Today, I spend my time developing leaders and working with leadership teams to help them thrive. My job is to surface the elephants in the room. To get 'nice' teams having tough conversations. This often involves some discomfort—giving feedback, talking through why some people's needs are being met while others are not. This work can be messy, but it is highly rewarding.

For those of you who have read my first book, *Thriving Leaders: Learn the Skills to Lead Confidently*, Chapter 2 discusses this very topic: Thriving Teams. This book builds on that model and goes deeper into what it takes to shift from dysfunctional, complacent, or performing teams to truly thriving teams. This book is designed to help teams shift from functioning to thriving—no matter where they sit today.

When I first decided to write this book, I wanted to conduct deep research on thriving teams. I hoped to replicate Google's Project Aristotle in a post-pandemic world, with organisations that were more relatable than Google is to most. When I started digging into what research had already been conducted in more recent years, there were so many studies to draw on. I soon realised it wasn't about creating yet another study. It was about synthesising this information into something digestible, interesting, and most importantly, applicable—so you can apply it to your own team.

From 2012 to 2014, Google conducted Project Aristotle, a study into 180 of its teams aimed at uncovering the secret to a highly effective team. Why do some teams achieve so much while others coast along?

The study examined 250 possible attributes, identifying patterns and behaviours within teams that led to high performance. The outcomes of the study found the following five attributes, in priority order:

1. **Psychological safety:** Team members feel safe to take risks and be vulnerable with each other.
2. **Dependability:** Team members get things done on time and meet Google's high bar for excellence.
3. **Team structure:** Team members have clear roles, plans, and goals.
4. **Meaning:** Work is personally important to team members.
5. **Impact:** Team members believe their work matters and creates change.

At the time, this study challenged conventional thinking about teams by highlighting the importance of psychological safety. Even though the concept of psychological safety had been introduced in a 1999 paper by Harvard Business School Professor of Leadership and Management Amy Edmondson, the concept gained traction after Google's research was published.

The part of the Project Aristotle research that is often *not* discussed is the areas that *did not* significantly correlate with team effectiveness at Google. These included team members sitting together in the same office, consensus decision-making, the extroversion of team members, individual performance of team members, workload size, team size, seniority, and tenure. These are areas that often get a lot of focus, but do not directly correlate to high performance.

A recent McKinsey study (2022–2024) analysed 14 annual literature reviews and over 140 published documents on effective teaming. The findings were then tested with 110 teams, comprising 905 team members over two years and across 42 countries. The research identified 17 health drivers of high-performing teams, including diverse perspectives, external orientation, role definition, commitment, goals and purpose, collaboration, communication, decision-making, feedback, meeting effectiveness, belonging, conflict management, innovative thinking, psychological safety, and trust. The study also found that high-performing teams demonstrate 11 of the 17 health factors. This shows that no team is perfect. Each team is different. Every team should continuously focus on how effectively they are operating.

Coincidentally—or perhaps not—all of these health drivers were already incorporated into the Thriving Teams Model, which was developed before the McKinsey study was conducted—further validation that I didn't need to conduct another two-year research study. Given the amount of thought leadership research and work with leadership teams I'd done, it is probably not a huge surprise.

So how do you take these factors out of the research papers and into your own team?

I start by asking teams to think of a time when they were part of a high-performing team. What made that team so great?

Typical responses include:

- **Clear goals and alignment:** Shared purpose and clear objectives.
- **Trust and psychological safety:** Mutual respect and a safe, supportive environment.
- **Strong communication:** Open, honest, and active listening.
- **Collaboration:** Strong relationships and teamwork.
- **Adaptability:** Flexibility and resilience under change and during crisis.
- **Accountability:** Defined roles and responsibilities, consistent follow-through.
- **Continuous improvement:** Learning, creativity, and problem-solving.
- **Positive culture:** Fun, energy, and celebrating successes.
- **Integrity:** Honest feedback, ethical behaviour, and no tolerance for toxicity.
- **Inclusivity:** Valuing diversity and individual strengths.

How would it feel if you were part of a team that incorporated all these elements?

Teams are not static. Even the highest-performing teams hit hurdles—team members leave, budgets get cut, and external factors impact people's ability to perform at their best.

Teams cannot succeed in isolation. They are part of a complex, adaptive system (Clutterbuck, 2019; Hawkins 2017). They need to interact, align, and collaborate with other teams and stakeholders—both internal and external to the organisation.

I wrote this book to answer some of the big questions that leaders ask themselves regularly:

- What makes a team high performing rather than average?
- How do you drive consistent outperformance without burning people out?
- How do teams become great when people are constantly coming and going?
- What practical things can you do to shift your team to thriving?
- How do you build psychological safety and trust within your team?
- How can your team work within an organisational system?
- How can your team have an impact and add value?
- How do you lead a high-performing team?

I aspire to empower leaders and teams to tackle their most difficult challenges—united, with a clear direction, so they can achieve their vision as a team. The more organisations that have thriving teams, the better workplaces will be.

Who this book is for

This book has been written for leaders of teams. It's incredibly challenging to be a leader in today's environment. You need to balance profitability, performance, engagement, and productivity. We live in a time where we are expected to do more with less, which is exhausting.

The economic climate is challenging for most organisations, with restructuring, cost-cutting, and downsizing. Technology is advancing at a rate that most individuals can't keep up with. The disruption caused by AI and cybersecurity developments means leaders and team members need to adapt, upskill, and integrate these changes into the way they work. If they don't, they will be left behind, and their teams will not succeed.

Workforce expectations are continually evolving. Hybrid work is here to stay, even though many organisations are mandating a return to the office. This shift is contributing to frustration, overwhelm, and uncertainty among employees.

Leadership roles are becoming less attractive. Australia is losing up to 500 managers to retirement per day, and in the USA, this number reaches 10,000 per day. Fewer people are aspiring to move into leadership positions—only 4% of the workforce has leadership aspirations.

According to Qualtrics' 2025 *Trends Report*, 38% of employees are experiencing pressure from their employers to increase productivity. This pressure stems from the pace of change, strategic shifts, external economic factors, and the introduction of AI. This is leading to employees feeling burnt out, let alone their leaders. In fact, one in three middle managers cited burnout as their biggest challenge (AHRI, 2024).

If you are a business owner, an executive, or a leader of a team, you all have one thing in common—well, perhaps more than one. For an organisation to be successful, the teams within it need to be successful. Good teams work together beyond their immediate functions. It's the daily choices and decisions made by leaders that drive progress towards the ultimate vision of the organisation. Rome wasn't built in a day, but they were laying bricks every day. When teams remain consistent and sustain focus on what's most important, their impact can be greater than anyone imagined.

If you are facing any of the following challenges with your team—or, more likely, multiple challenges—then this book is for you:

- **Team productivity:** Is your team operating as effectively as it should? Are they focusing on the right priorities, or are they unproductive?
- **Breaking down silos:** Teams, functions, and departments often operate in silos. High-performing individuals may focus on their own responsibilities, neglecting the benefits of cross-functional collaboration and horizontal leadership. How aligned is your team on collective accountabilities?
- **Balancing strategy with operations:** Teams often react to immediate needs rather than thinking ahead. Are there clear strategies in place, or do competing priorities dominate?
- **Interpersonal dynamics:** Personality styles and diverse team dynamics can create challenges. Do different personalities and work styles lead to friction or conflict within your team?
- **Decision-making:** Does your team avoid making tough choices, or do they suffer from decision fatigue? Are they collaborating effectively on decisions, or does everything default to the leader?
- **Navigating change:** With increasing complexity and rapid change, maintaining team productivity is difficult. Many industries face rolling restructures, uncertain budgets, and temporary roles, leading to stress and instability.
- **Risk of burnout:** Blurred boundaries in hybrid models, relentless pressure to deliver more, and excessive workloads put leaders and teams at risk of burnout.
- **'Nice' team culture:** Some teams struggle with passive cultures where difficult conversations don't happen. A 'nice' culture arises when people avoid conflict to spare feelings.

- **Entitlement culture:** Where individuals believe the leader or organisation owes them something.
- **Stakeholder expectations:** Aligning with key stakeholders can be a challenge, especially when conflicting priorities arise.
- **Lack of feedback:** Does feedback only come from the leader, rather than within the team?
- **Lack of accountability:** Without peer accountability, team performance suffers.
- **Collective accountability:** What is the team collectively accountable for? Do they follow through on commitments and hold each other accountable?
- **Avoiding direct communication:** Do team members bring complaints about their peers to you instead of addressing them directly?
- **Managing toxic team members:** Is there one difficult individual making it hard for the rest of the team to move forward collectively? Do they create drama, operate in isolation, or play people off against each other?
- **Building cohesion in hybrid teams:** How well does your team collaborate across different locations and remote work arrangements?

Leading a thriving team means showing up—even when it's hard. Especially when it's hard. It means having the courage to face what's not working, to back your people while holding the bar high, and to keep learning how to do both at the same time.

Leaders cast a long shadow. You are being observed—whether you realise it or not—and that shadow shapes how safe, how motivated, and how accountable your team feels. You don't need to be perfect, but you do need to be present, intentional, and self-aware.

It would be great if you could tick a box that says, "Now I'm a great leader." But just like teamwork, it is continual and ongoing.

If you want to learn more, I wrote a whole book on this topic, *Thriving Leaders*.

Leadership is an action, and we can all demonstrate leadership even if we don't have formal authority. This book is also valuable for team members. Every team member contributes to the team dynamic. Teamwork is inherently messy, and we are all part of the mess.

Why read this book

The Thriving Teams Model improves team performance, engagement, and productivity, leading to measurable business results. By understanding what is currently working well within your team and where improvements are needed, you can implement proven strategies to address dysfunction and build a thriving team.

This book also helps teams collaborate more effectively, understand and value each other's similarities and differences, and promote innovation and learning. Team members feel connected, united, valued, and motivated. There is a sense of empowerment, trust, respect, and collective fulfilment.

There is extensive research on the benefits of working in a thriving team. This includes improved productivity, reduced turnover, cost and time savings through efficiencies, improved employee engagement, and better business results including profitability. But don't just take my word for it. Below are some of the stats and measures of successful team effectiveness, and why this is so damn important if you want your organisation to succeed.

Gallup's 2024 *State of the Global Workplace Report* found that only 21% of employees are engaged at work globally—a decline from 23% in 2023—costing the global economy approximately US $438 billion in lost productivity. That's a big number! In Australia and New

Zealand only 23% of employees are thriving at work and engaged, meaning that 77% are not engaged or are actively disengaged. This costs the Australian economy AU$211 billion per year, according to the Australian Human Resources Institute (2024).

The relationship between engagement at work and organisational outcomes is measured in Gallup's *Q12 Meta-Analysis* released in 2025. This study found that highly engaged teams are 23% more profitable than those with low engagement. Highly engaged teams experience 51% lower turnover in low-turnover industries and 21% lower turnover in high-turnover industries. Engaged teams are less likely to leave, improving retention as people want to stay. Not to mention the cost to recruit a new team member and the lead time to both technical and cultural competency.

Thriving teams make good business sense! Not to mention the less tangible benefits—improved connection, trust and fulfilment among team members, and teams that feel valued, enjoy their work, and take pride in their contributions.

Throughout this book, I draw on extensive research on high-performing teams and leadership. I have also interviewed thought leaders who have inspired my work, all experts in their fields: Amy Edmondson, David Clutterbuck, Dermot Crowley, Claire DeCarteret, Kaye-Monk Morgan, Grant Gemmell, Justin Williams, and Leo Bottary. I've also provided Real-world Case Studies and Teams in Practice so you can understand how this relates in your world. These interviews are available on the *Thriving Leaders Podcast*.

How to use this book

This book is a practical guide designed to help you reflect on your team dynamics, uncover what's really happening, and examine your role as a leader in shaping those interactions. Leadership isn't just about directing—it's about self-awareness and understanding how your actions contribute to the culture of your team. Every member plays a role in shaping the team's environment, and this book will help you navigate those dynamics with intention.

To support your learning, each chapter includes tangible activities and conversation prompts that you can work on with your team over time. You'll also find QR codes, providing access to additional resources to help embed these practices into your leadership approach, including a Thriving Teams Diagnostic that measures where your team is: dysfunctional, complacent, performing, or thriving. This tool is great to assess where you are today, track progress, and revisit action plans, ensuring that your team's development remains a priority.

Most of the strategies in this book require only an investment of time, arguably your most precious resource. Leadership growth doesn't always require big budgets or complex programs; sometimes, the most impactful changes come from consistent, thoughtful conversations and small, intentional shifts in the way you lead.

When reading this book, reflect on where your team is. Think about the team you lead, as well as the team that you are part of. It is likely that different teams will be in different stages. Use these insights to meet each team where it is—and guide it to where it has the potential to be.

CHAPTER 1

Thriving Teams

Thriving teams are made by the people in them. It's about being with people you respect. You're adding value to each other and collectively adding value to the team.

— David Clutterbuck, on the *Thriving Leaders Podcast*

What is a team?

Just because you are called a team doesn't mean you are one.

Both teams and groups have their place in organisations. It is important, however, to be clear about the differences and distinctions so that you can interact intentionally.

A team is "... a small number of people with complementary skills, who are committed to a common purpose, performance goals and approach, for which they hold themselves mutually accountable" (Katzenbach, 1994). A group is a collection of individuals who perform based on individual contributions.

Characteristics of a group:

- **Stand-alone goals:** Each member may have separate, individual goals. Members are generally independent in their work and responsibilities. Performance is generally measured by the sum of individual achievements rather than cohesive outcomes.

- **No collective purpose:** There's no single, unifying purpose. The task and deliverables drive the group.
- **Individual accountability:** Responsibility lies solely with the individual for their own outcomes. They are responsible for their own performance.
- **Cooperation:** Members support each other but do not necessarily engage deeply in collaborative efforts. The output is often the aggregate of individual contributions.

A group is useful when quick action is needed and draws on specialist expertise. It is great for short-term projects that require quick decision-making. Solutions are often more unique, as members have independent perspectives and are less likely to conform. Groups often refer to themselves as a team, as there is a perceived positive status of being a team.

Characteristics of a team:

- **Shared goals:** Everyone is aligned towards common objectives. Each team member has a specific role, and there is interdependence and collective performance. (See Chapter 6 – Clear Direction)
- **Collective purpose:** There is a unified purpose driving every team member that unites and binds them together. (See Chapter 2 – Team Purpose)
- **Individual and shared accountability:** Each person is responsible for their own tasks and the team's overall success. Members hold each other accountable to achieve team goals. There is shared responsibility and ownership of outcomes. (See Chapter 7 – Team Accountability)

- **Collaboration:** Team members actively seek each other's involvement and input. Team members leverage each other's strengths for problem-solving and decision-making. (See Chapter 12 – Team Alignment)

A team is valuable when an organisation needs to solve complex problems, collaborate long term, complete interdependent tasks, and improve productivity.

When working with larger teams, one of the key distinctions we often explore is the difference between a team and a group. Understanding this difference is crucial, as it significantly influences how you operate and achieve your goals.

The reality is that whether you are a team or a group, it won't always be clear-cut. Think about teams and groups lying on a continuum rather than being binary. As leaders, gaining clarity on whether your people are functioning as a team or a group is essential. This understanding shapes your approach, commitment, and ultimately, your success.

Types of teams

There are many ways to categorise the types of teams that exist within organisations. Edmondson (1999) examines teams across different spectrums: cross-functional to single-function, time-limited to enduring, and manager-led to self-led.

Cross-functional teams consist of members from different departments. This is often the case in leadership teams, where support functions are combined with the core function of the team. Functional teams, on the other hand, are based on expertise—for example, a marketing team where all members have similar skills and specialisations.

Time-limited teams, such as project or agile-based teams, focus on specific deliverables over a set period. In contrast, business-as-usual teams are enduring.

Manager-led teams exist in most organisational structures where hierarchy is valued, whereas self-led teams are self-organising and operate with shared accountability and decision-making.

More recently, teams have evolved and are shifting away from traditional hierarchies. They often are more dynamic, such as matrixed teams, which have dual reporting lines. In this book, I use the terms teams and leadership teams interchangeably. The core difference lies in their position within an organisation and the level of authority they hold. Leadership teams may be the most senior team in the organisation. Or, in larger organisations, they may exist at multiple levels. Leadership teams set strategic direction and make key decisions.

Team size

Size doesn't matter. It's how you use it.

The optimal team size is a question I regularly get asked, especially by leaders of large teams. Most research suggests the ideal team size is between four and seven people. However, there are many variables—different types of teams and different team purposes—that need to be considered. The research is often conflicting.

In *Decide and Deliver*, Bain & Company shares that when a team size exceeds seven people, decision-making is reduced by 10% for every additional person. This means that if you have 10 people on your leadership team, decision-making is diminished by 30%, and in a team of 12, it's reduced by 50%. If your team doesn't need to meet regularly to make major decisions, a larger team may work better for you—for example, in a call centre environment.

Amazon's Jeff Bezos has a widely cited two-pizza rule, where every internal team should be small enough to be fed by two pizzas (hopefully, nobody has too big an appetite). This rule was designed to enhance efficiency and scalability—smaller teams get things done faster and spend more time on what truly matters.

However, in the book *Working Backwards*, two former Amazon executives, Bill Carr and Colin Bryar, share how they evolved beyond the two-pizza rule. While it proved useful for product teams, some projects required larger teams. They found that a better predictor of team success was a leader with the right skills, experience, authority, and a singular focus—a concept known as single-thread leadership.

Harvard researcher J. Richard Hackman states that "four to six members is the best team size for most tasks, that no work team should have more than 10 members, and that performance problems and interpersonal friction increase exponentially as team size grows".

Smaller teams enable quicker and more efficient decision-making as they can collaborate more efficiently. There's increased accountability, as team members are more invested in the team's success, and it's easier to hold each other accountable since responsibilities are clearer.

Larger teams tend to get distracted. There are too many cooks in the kitchen. There is a greater likelihood of interpersonal differences as there are just more people. When we overextend spans of control, we dilute responsibility and a sense of belonging.

What do you do if you are leading a big team? If you are leading a large team and keep questioning whether it's too big—or if your team members are raising concerns—you probably already know the answer. It may be time to make some hard decisions about who really needs to be at the table.

If you are part of a large team, chances are the challenges have not gone unnoticed by your team. Have an open conversation about the pros and cons of your team size. Address the elephant in the room. If the decision is to remain a large team, ensure there is clarity about how it operates. For example, the full team may come together for strategy, culture, and people discussions, while a core team focuses on sales and commercial decisions.

Teams work best when they are:

- Small enough to make decisions efficiently and collaborate effectively.
- Large enough to bring together diverse skill sets, perspectives, and expertise.

While there is no perfect number, having a clear team purpose along with defined roles and responsibilities can help determine the optimal size. If decision-making, accountability, or communication are suffering due to a large team, it might be time to re-evaluate. However, changing the size or composition of a team should solve the right problem—so ask yourself: What issue are we actually solving?

Team dynamics

Every team has its own vibe—shaped by who's in it, how they behave, and what they're trying to achieve. The leader sets the tone more than anyone, whether they realise it or not. Team dynamics are fluid, so as a leader, your job is to read the room, spot the tension early, and step in when you observe unhelpful behaviours.

Diversity—of background, thinking, age, gender, culture—drives innovation, because different perspectives challenge assumptions and reduce the risk of groupthink. But difference without understanding can cause friction. When people don't accept or respect each other's styles or perspectives, it opens the door to poor behaviour and politics.

Toxic dynamics—like passive aggression, micromanagement, bullying, gossip, or even just unchecked ego—can break a team. One rotten egg can ruin the whole omelette. It might be easy to blame individuals, but every team member contributes to the culture. A toxic team environment is not sustainable. As the leader, it's your job to confront poor behaviour head-on while staying curious about what's underneath it. What's driving this person? What's being threatened?

This behaviour may stem from all team members, a few, or even just one individual. It is easy to point fingers or assign blame, but as a leader, it is your responsibility to address the behaviour directly. However, every team member contributes to the overall dynamic, and there may be underlying reasons for certain behaviours. Approach these situations with curiosity. Don't let dysfunction derail your team.

When dysfunction sits at the top, it filters through the entire organisation. It shapes the culture, informs how priorities are set, affects how decisions are made, and ultimately impacts performance. If senior leaders are misaligned, dodging accountability, avoiding tough conversations, or stuck in silos, that behaviour ripples outwards. The result? Mistrust, confusion, and disengagement.

Take the time to address misalignment, encourage open communication, and rebuild trust. The payoff is significant. It begins with alignment of purpose, relationships, and accountability.

The good news is positive team dynamics ripple through organisations too. When teams have each other's backs, challenge each other with respect, and embrace learning, they create momentum that's hard to stop. Strong team dynamics are the foundation of a high-performing team.

Teamwork makes the dream work. How much of a team player are you?

What is a thriving team?

A thriving team is high performing, engaged, and productive. A thriving team focuses on its common purpose and goals. Team members work together through strong relationships and shared accountability to innovate and deliver exceptional business results.

There are four states that a team may be operating in: dysfunctional, complacent, performing, or thriving. Teams move between these states as they evolve. It is also not a linear model; teams progress and digress through different triggers, situations, and contexts.

Dysfunctional

Dysfunctional teams often occur when the team doesn't have the capability or motivation to perform. Team members avoid each other and the tough conversations. There is often politics, toxicity, and individuals driving their own agendas. This team is disengaged and lacks motivation or cohesion as a team. There is a lack of accountability and a sense of overwhelm. Team members are emotionally detached from the organisation, team, or work. The team feels unmotivated, frustrated, detached, disinterested, isolated, removed, or disconnected.

Complacent

Complacent teams are cruising along, often because they have been in the team or role for a long time. They meet basic expectations but lack drive and initiative to do more. Often team members have withdrawn from the team to deliver the expectations of their job, which leads to them operating in silos rather than collaborating. They don't feel challenged and may resist change as they are used to the status quo. The team feels passive, compliant, settled, stagnant, or indifferent.

Performing

Performing teams are consistent, reliable, and meet expectations. Collectively, the team is getting the job done and operates well together to meet standards. There is a sense of competence, professionalism, and respect for each other. However, they may not be innovating, pushing boundaries, or exceeding expectations. The team is functional and productive but lacks motivation to go above and beyond. It feels competent, reliable, capable, consistent, steady, or effective.

Thriving

Thriving teams are high performing. There is a sense of connection to the purpose, deep trust, strong relationships, and a sense of accountability. The team is engaged and cares about their work and the organisation. The team exceeds expectations in terms of business performance. It feels motivated, purposeful, empowered, unified, collaborative, cohesive, dedicated, committed, loyal, inspired, or passionate.

It's important to note that teams are not defined by high performance. Focusing solely on performance can have unintended negative impacts. Instead, we need to consider teams holistically, systemically, and emotionally.

Teamwork is an evolution.

Thriving Teams Model

The Thriving Teams Model is based on extensive experience creating effective teams, empirical research, and evolving thought leadership on high-performing teams. The saying, standing on the shoulders of giants, gets overused. However, it is true in the context of the research on thriving teams.

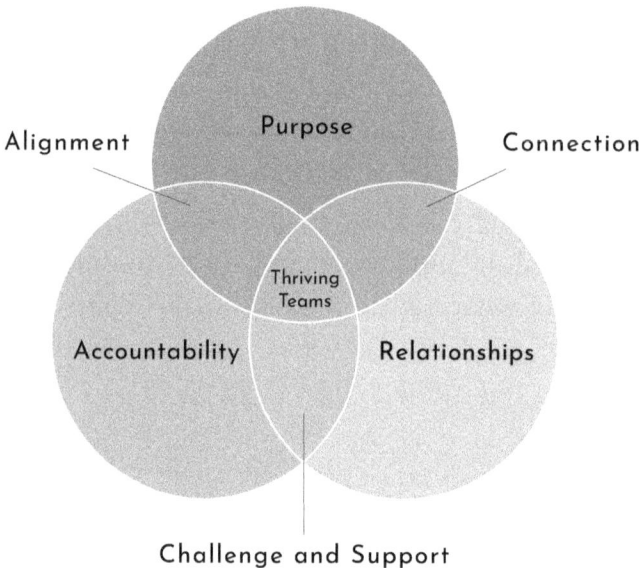

There are three fundamental components of a thriving team:

- **Purpose: Why** the team exists.
- **Relationships: How** the team works together.
- **Accountability: What** the team will achieve and by **when**.

The intersection between these components is equally as important:

- **Connection:** Togetherness and team processes.
- **Challenge and support:** Healthy debate and learning.
- **Alignment:** Team and stakeholder.

Thriving teams have a clear team purpose and meaningful work, where the team understands who is accountable for what and how to leverage the strengths of the team. This helps to develop strong relationships through psychological safety and trust, so team members feel like they belong. They are clear on the direction they are headed, they are accountable to each other, and they can hold each other accountable to this. The team is connected; they have simple team processes and ways of working that are reviewed for effectiveness regularly. They have a strong sense of togetherness beyond the work, and get to know each other on a human level. They have healthy, challenging debates and get everything on the table that needs to be said. They learn from the mistakes and successes as a team and support one another. They are aligned and committed to the direction of the team. They gain alignment with stakeholders, both internal and external, and build strong stakeholder relationships.

These elements are not static. Teams will evolve, lapse, face challenges, regress, and continue to evolve again. It's about making progress as a team. If you notice that your team needs a reset, or if you have new team members join, it is often time to reassess where you need to focus. This could be getting the team to complete the Thriving Teams Diagnostic, to identify areas that require focus. One-on-one conversations, if psychological safety is low. Or team discussions so you can hear different perspectives.

Teamwork is real work. It is hard. It is messy. It requires tough conversations. It involves discomfort that drives us to be better for the greater good of the team. It is also fun, energising, empowering, and inspiring to be part of a thriving team.

One Team

You are likely part of more than one team. This is common in functional and cross-functional teams, that have matrix models, such as support functions like Finance, Risk, Human Resources, and Marketing.

In my 10 years at the National Australia Bank, I held various People & Culture (P&C) roles. There were many times as a P&C Business Partner where I sat on the leadership team of a Business Unit which I supported, and was also part of the P&C team. This dual role meant that I spent most of my time with my client group, so at times I felt more connected to them, despite my 'hard' reporting line into P&C. Then in different roles when supporting other client groups, I felt the opposite, more part of the P&C team. At times I felt torn between two teams. I see this commonly now with clients, who feel they need to side on particular issues when it is convenient for them to do so. This creates an 'us vs them' dynamic.

In his book *The Five Dysfunctions of a Team*, leadership expert Patrick Lencioni introduces the concept of a first or primary team. Is this the team that you lead, or the team that you are part of? Lencioni suggests that your first team should be the team you are part of or the more senior team. Most leaders instinctively view their first team as the one they lead, as they feel most accountable to it and spend more of their time with this team. However, this mindset can drive siloed behaviour, where leaders focus on protecting their own patch rather than contributing to the greater good of the organisation.

Rather than seeing this as an 'either/or' decision, I encourage leaders to see it as an 'and'. The reality is you still need to work effectively in the team you lead *and* the team you are part of. There is no room for 'us vs them'.

Instead of picking a favourite team—much like trying to pick a favourite child—the goal should be to create a One Team mindset. Leaders who adopt this approach make decisions that benefit the entire organisation, rather than just their own patch, team, business unit, or department. A One Team mindset breaks down silos, which are so common in teams. This means team members make decisions for the greater good of the whole.

When we travel overseas, we naturally slow down, take in the scenery, admire the architecture, and immerse ourselves in history and culture. Yet, in our daily lives, we often operate on autopilot, rarely stopping to look around or appreciate our surroundings.

The same applies to teams. High-performing individuals can develop tunnel vision, focusing only on their own area, which leads to siloed behaviour. Thriving teams, however, lift their gaze and see the bigger picture. They make decisions that benefit the entire organisation, not just their immediate function.

How can you help your team lift their gaze?

Many organisations have strong individuals who are highly effective in their roles, but that alone does not create high-performing teams. Leaders must encourage their teams to take a broader perspective, ensuring decisions align with organisational goals rather than individual or department priorities.

A thriving team understands that collective success outweighs individual gains. The challenge for leaders is to cultivate this mindset, ensuring that every team member recognises their role in achieving the bigger picture.

Leading a thriving team

Leading a thriving team requires curiosity and clarity. I believe that as the leader, you need to be a facilitator and a team coach.

There are so many instances with your team where you play the role of facilitator, whether that's facilitating team meetings, cross-functional workshops with stakeholders, team-goal, or strategy setting. This means you need to develop the skill to facilitate with confidence and draw out the wisdom from the team. The power in thriving teams is the collective knowledge and expertise of each team member. When we are operating as a facilitator, we are creating a space for reflection, collaboration, and decision-making to reach an outcome.

The good news is that it's not all on you. In a thriving team, all team members feel empowered to make decisions and be involved. Everyone must lead. Distributed leadership is a model where decision-making and authority are shared. It requires interdependent actions, collective input, and autonomy. The real value comes from harnessing collective intelligence and learning while maintaining structure and accountability. The leader, in the ultimate position of authority, acts as a facilitator who enables the team to contribute their best knowledge, skills, and ideas. This often extends beyond the team itself and builds the networks required to innovate and solve complex problems. Distributed leadership enhances decision-making, productivity, and creativity, and is linked to greater employee engagement and ownership—as people feel empowered in their roles.

When the leader operates as team coach they develop the collective system over time. They ask curious questions, share observations, reflect, and provide feedback. They help the team understand their dynamics, highlight patterns of behaviour, and illuminate how the team makes decisions. There is a whole chapter in *Thriving Leaders* dedicated to building the skill to coach. (See Chapter 10 – Healthy Debate in this book to learn more about asking curious questions)

Thriving Teams

A thriving team is more than just a group of high-performing individuals—it is a cohesive, engaged, and purpose-driven unit that collaborates, challenges, and holds each other accountable. Teams evolve through different states—dysfunctional, complacent, performing, and thriving—shifting based on their environment, challenges, and leadership.

A key distinction in organisations is the difference between teams and groups. A thriving team has a clear purpose, strong relationships, and the team can hold each other accountable. That way you can unite to achieve collective success.

Teams are not static—they evolve, lapse, regress, progress, and grow. The best teams continuously assess their effectiveness and make the necessary adjustments to improve. Teamwork requires effort.

Thriving teams demonstrate the following core elements, which will be discussed in detail in the following parts of this book.

- **Purpose: Why** the team exists.
- **Relationships: How** the team works together.
- **Accountability: What** the team will achieve and by **when**.
- **Connection:** Togetherness and team processes.
- **Challenge and support:** Healthy debate and learning.
- **Alignment:** Team and stakeholder.

A thriving team doesn't happen by chance—it is intentionally built and nurtured over time. Leaders set the tone, but every team member plays a role in shaping teams' effectiveness. When teams operate with clarity, connection, and commitment, they don't just perform—they thrive.

Actions

1. **Assess whether you are a team or a group.** Determine whether the team functions as a team or a group. Discuss with your team. If you realise you're operating more like a group (especially if the team is large), talk through the differences between a group and a team. Ask:
   - Are we a team or a group?
   - What characteristics indicate our choice?
   - How much of a team do we want, or need, to be?
   - If we want to operate more as a team, what do we need to do more or less of?

2. **Assess team composition and size.** Is the team set up for success in terms of composition, skills, size, and ways of working? If the answer is no, reflect on the following questions:
   - Who should be in the team?
   - Do all voices get heard, or does time limit discussions?
   - Is my team the right mix of skills, perspectives, and expertise to achieve our goals?
   - Is my team the appropriate size to make decisions, collaborate effectively, and encourage diverse perspectives?

3. **Complete the Thriving Teams Diagnostic.** QR code below. Where is your team today? Are they dysfunctional, complacent, performing, or thriving?

   Share the results with the team. Ask:
   - What are the strengths in the team?
   - What are the areas for improvement?
   - Where should we focus?

4. **Build a One Team mindset.** Help your team lift their gaze beyond the day-to-day. Build connection to the bigger picture. Ask:

    - What gets in the way of us operating as One Team?
    - What actions or behaviours would we demonstrate if we were One Team?

5. **Build your leadership skills as a facilitator and coach.** Practise asking more what or how questions. Leverage the wisdom in your team to achieve outcomes. There are tips throughout this book to help build your facilitation and coaching skills.

RESOURCES

www.thrivingculture.com.au/ttbook

PART 1

Purpose

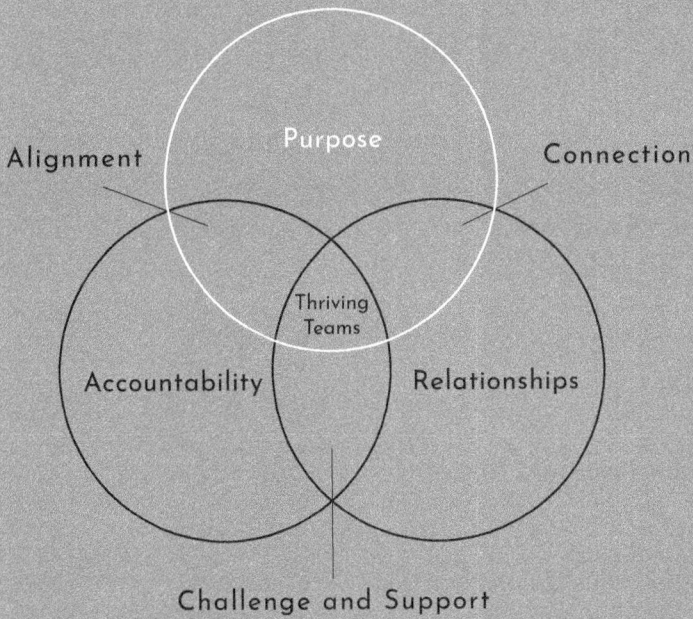

Alignment

Purpose

Connection

Thriving
Teams

Accountability

Relationships

Challenge and Support

Purpose relates to an intention, a core belief, and a reason for being. A purpose is why you exist. It should be meaningful, aspirational, and motivating. A purpose is often bigger or has an impact beyond the individual.

In the Thriving Teams Model, Purpose intersects with Alignment and Connection. When the team connects with each other, it needs to be meaningful and purposeful. The team has clarity and is aligned on its purpose. In thriving teams, focusing on the team's purpose and meaningful work is critical.

One of the most iconic books of the 20th century is Viktor Frankl's *Man's Search for Meaning*. A Jewish psychiatrist who is separated from his family, including his pregnant wife, Frankl shares his experience of living in a concentration camp under the Nazi regime. Frankl survived this experience; his family did not. He observed that when people have meaning and purpose, they can withstand unimaginable challenges and remain resilient in the toughest times. If we translate that into our everyday lives, we should focus on finding meaning, as this is the path to fulfilment and happiness.

There are four levels of purpose to which individuals can connect at work:

1. Organisational purpose

An organisation's purpose is why it exists. It should have meaning so that employees feel connected to it. As leaders, it is our role to help connect our people to the organisation's purpose. By linking what is important to them and their individual values to those of the organisation, employees feel a sense of belonging. Purpose-led cultures are becoming more attractive to employees as it gives them meaning. (See Chapter 6 – Clear Direction on how to create a strategy)

2. Team purpose

A clear team purpose binds the team to a common 'why'. Almost all literature on high-performing teams describes the need for a collective team purpose. The team purpose defines why the team exists and connects team members. (See Chapter 2 – Team Purpose)

3. Meaningful work

People want to make a difference, which makes them take pride in their work. The more an individual can connect to the work and the value that their work provides, the more rewarding their work will be. As leaders, we need to help teams make a connection between their work and its impact. (See Chapter 3 – Meaningful Work)

4. Personal values

We each have core values that are important to us. These could be family, social, relational, or environmental. Our values shape our decisions and influence our beliefs and assumptions. (See Chapter 8 – Togetherness)

This part of the book explores team purpose and meaningful work.

CHAPTER 2

Team Purpose

Life is never made unbearable by circumstances,
but only by lack of meaning and purpose.
— Viktor Frankl

⊕ **REAL-WORLD CASE STUDY**

Hive Legal—Leading with purpose and redefining legal practice

Hive Legal is widely recognised as one of Australia's most progressive legal practices. Built on flexible work, value-based pricing, and design thinking, Hive has replaced many of the traditional hallmarks of professional services—such as billable hours and time sheets—with a model that fosters teamwork, collaboration, and client trust.

This innovative approach has driven strong performance and industry recognition, including awards for excellence in commercial law, employer of choice, innovation, and health and wellbeing.

From its inception in 2014, Hive Legal has been purpose-driven. *"What makes us different is why we do it and the way that we do it,"* said Principal Joanna Green. *"We deliver our services as a team, we engage with our clients with empathy and build ongoing relationships."*

As the business matured over the past decade, so did its sense of purpose. *"We felt like we'd moved beyond the initial disruption phase,"* explained Executive Director and Experience Designer Melissa Lyon. *"So, we refreshed our purpose to focus on the positive impact we want to make—not just for clients and our team, but for the broader community. Our purpose now is 'to create, enable, and inspire positive impacts through high-quality and progressive services'."*

Hive Legal's purpose operates at multiple levels:

- Organisational: An overarching purpose, recently refreshed to ensure it remains meaningful 10 years on.
- Team: Clarity on how each team contributes to the organisational purpose.
- Individual: Connecting to what motivates each person to contribute to Hive's success.

The evolution of Hive's purpose demonstrates that it is not static. It evolves—and when teams pause to reconnect with it, performance, alignment, and engagement all lift. As Hive Legal's experience shows, purpose requires ongoing attention.

Why a team purpose

A clear team purpose binds a team together with a common 'why'. When your team share a purpose, they function with clarity, direction, and impact—and that filters down to every level of the organisation.

The organisation's purpose and the team's purpose will align, but are different. Even if you're the most senior leadership team in the organisation, your team's purpose will be distinct from the organisation's purpose. There will likely be a connection between the two or they will be complementary.

It doesn't matter whether you're a newly formed team or one that's been working together for years—having a defined team purpose is crucial. This isn't about setting goals or defining a mission. Yes, your team needs a clear direction, whether that's a strategy or goals (see Chapter 6 – Clear Direction), but that's different from purpose. The purpose is deeper—it's about meaning. A team's purpose is your collective 'why'.

As a team, finding collective meaning is a powerful process. A team's purpose is more than just a statement; it is why you exist and what binds you together. It's not enough to just write down a team purpose—you have to bring it to life through everyday actions, conversations, and decision-making. And, just as importantly, hold each other accountable to it. That's when purpose strengthens a team.

A 2024 *Harvard Business Review* article, 'Stop Wasting Valuable Time', highlighted that streamlined work and well-defined team purposes and charters help to speed up decision-making and make meetings more efficient by up to 40%.

⚙ TEAM IN PRACTICE

Reinvigorating a siloed and complacent team

An Executive Director in the State Government was leading a large group of functional heads. Each leader was effective in their own patch, but the team wasn't operating as a collective. Monthly meetings had become dominated by lengthy updates, leaving little space for decision-making or tackling shared challenges. The group was busy but not cohesive, and the lack of alignment was starting to impact outcomes.

The team had drifted into complacency, with everyone working comfortably within their silos. Collaboration was minimal, and when things went wrong, finger-pointing and blame were more common than problem-solving. Risk-taking was rare, and a fixed mindset of "we've always done it this way" blocked fresh thinking. Long tenure in roles reinforced old patterns rather than creating momentum for change. The team only seemed to unite in times of crisis, but this wasn't sustainable.

The Executive Director grew increasingly frustrated with the lack of collaboration. Attempts to push the group into more strategic conversations fell flat. Here's how they put it:

- "We're not working as one team—we're just a collection of updates."
- "Team members are hesitant to take risks."
- "Some have been in this group for too long, reinforcing old patterns."

A reset was needed. They created a team purpose and discussed what behaviours they needed to demonstrate to have a One Team mindset. This informed their team values. Meetings shifted from information updates to decision-making. The Executive Director created a stronger sense of accountability and alignment by co-creating shared goals for the unit. The group began to collaborate on shared priorities, tackle problems collectively, and shift away from the blame culture. This not only reinvigorated the team but also built momentum for innovation across their portfolios.

The more senior you are in an organisation, or the bigger and more siloed the business, the more fragmented team functions can become. For some teams, finding a shared purpose can feel impossible, especially if you've been thrown together through multiple restructures. However, this is where purpose really matters. Without it, teams operate in silos, pulling in different directions, making collaboration harder. With it, alignment happens, decisions become clearer, and work becomes more meaningful.

Ever noticed how teams suddenly pull together in a crisis? That's because they have a shared purpose and a clear goal. Personal agendas and differences take a back seat, and the focus sharpens. Going through tough times together also strengthens relationships—people feel like they've got each other's backs. It's like a magnetic force pulling everyone in the same direction. Some teams only find their rhythm in a crisis. When things are calm, they default back to silos—high-performing individuals working in isolation. And that's not sustainable.

Teams that operate in constant firefighting mode will eventually burn out. Your team culture isn't sustainable if you're only cohesive under pressure. Instead, build that same sense of alignment and urgency *before* a crisis. A well-defined team purpose helps make that shift.

How to create a team purpose

As motivational speaker Simon Sinek suggests, we should "start with why". This is always a great place to start with a team—discussing, brainstorming, agreeing, and then committing to the team's purpose.

Cultivate the environment

Create the right environment and space to discuss your team's purpose. Carve out enough time so that the conversation isn't rushed. Find time outside of the day-to-day operations to have a rich dialogue about team purpose. Don't just tag it on as an additional agenda item in an existing meeting. It needs space. I'd suggest one hour to 90 minutes to do it justice.

Connection

Start with a connection exercise, where the team has the opportunity to get to know each other better. Chad Littlefield, facilitator extraordinaire, calls it "connection before content".

Ask each team member to share what they are most proud of as a team. Capture what is said on a whiteboard, flipchart, or online shared document. Now that the team has established a deeper connection, you are ready to start the conversation about purpose.

Co-create your purpose

Set the scene by explaining that you will co-create a meaningful team purpose, where everyone contributes, and it is team-owned. The intent is to open the door to meaningful dialogue and help individuals find purpose in their work.

Work with your team to articulate a team purpose statement. It should be one sentence that describes why your team exists. It should be inspiring. It should connect the team. A clear team purpose is key to a thriving team.

Questions to help you develop a team purpose include:

- Why does our team exist?
- Why does our work matter?
- What impact does our team have?
- What would happen if this team didn't exist?

Use a whiteboard and two different-coloured markers. Start by capturing responses to the questions above. If using Post-it Notes, ask team members to write down one idea per note, and then group them into themes. Once all ideas are exhausted, use the second colour marker to highlight words or phrases that resonate most by underlining them. From there, refine and craft a concise purpose statement that feels right for the team.

Tips for crafting a purpose statement:

- Keep it concise. You don't want the world's longest. Otherwise, nobody will remember it.
- Avoid corporate jargon or vague wording that could apply to any team.
- Move beyond what the team does and focus on *why* they do it—think about the meaning, impact, and beliefs driving them.
- Always check in with everyone that the team's purpose resonates. Ask questions like "When you say it out loud, does it feel energising, aspirational, or motivating?" or "Does this feel like our collective team's purpose?"
- AI tools can be useful for refining the final statement but ensure the team is actively engaged in the process. It should be their statement, something they connect with—not just an AI-generated one.

Here are some example team purpose statements:

- To empower our people to innovate and deliver meaningful outcomes for our customers.
- Lead and influence positive change in the communities we serve.
- We deliver high-quality outcomes for clients through connected, values-led leadership.
- To create an environment where our people can do their best work and raise the standards of our industry.

Facilitation considerations

Use tools effectively, whether that's whiteboards, flipcharts, Post-it Notes, and other visual aids if you are together. Or digital whiteboards, chat functions, and polling when online.

Build in time for consolidation of what has been discussed or learned. This may be individual reflections and then team discussions.

Team values

A purpose statement means nothing unless you live and breathe it every day. This means that you need to understand how it influences your team's values and behaviours. Individually, everyone has personal values, but collectively, the team must define its shared values.

A great starting point is asking team members to share their personal values or completing the free Values In Action (VIA) Character Strengths Survey and discussing the top five results. The VIA survey is a great free tool based on the work of positive psychology researchers Martin Seligman and Christian Peterson. You may identify some super strengths and collective values from doing this exercise. You can discuss the similarities, differences, and collective strengths within the team.

Values need behavioural descriptors so they become observable, actionable, and something team members can hold each other accountable to. We need to live up to our values. If it is vague or just a word, it becomes meaningless.

Here are some questions to help define your collective values:

- What core values support our purpose?
- What behaviours help us perform at our best?
- What behaviours are we not demonstrating that would help us thrive as a team?
- What behaviours would help us work better together?

Tips for defining team values:

- Less is more—focus on three core values that truly matter. People can't remember more than three things.

- Choose values that you want to see the team do more of, rather than behaviours that the team already demonstrate consistently.
- The team needs to be open to calling each other out when they are not demonstrating the agreed values. Accountability for upholding values is key.
- Create mechanisms for feedback when team members are demonstrating or not demonstrating the values.
- Check in with the team to see if these values will help us live our purpose as a team. Refine accordingly.

Example values:

- **One Team:** We make decisions for the greater good and present a united front.
- **Feedback:** We give and receive feedback openly.
- **Presence:** We are engaged, proactive, and contribute meaningfully.
- **Honesty:** We communicate transparently and challenge ideas respectfully.
- **Accountability:** We do what we say we will do.

This structured approach ensures that purpose and values are clearly defined.

Living your purpose and values

We want to ensure that purpose and values are not treated as a one-off exercise but instead become something truly impactful. They must become ingrained in the team's daily work, driving alignment, motivation, and focus.

Make them visible: Keep them front of mind by including them on meeting agendas, displaying them in the workspace, in meeting rooms, on desks, or integrating them into collaboration tools like Teams or Slack.

Set the rhythm: Integrate them into your meeting cadence. Begin meetings with an example of how the team has lived their purpose that week. Rotate the meeting chair as it involves more members of the team, and helps with distributed leadership within the team. It also helps stop meetings from stagnating.

Peer accountability: Have a rotating observer in your team meeting. Their role is to observe how you are living your values in the meeting. In the last five minutes of the meeting, the meeting observer gives feedback to the team on how well the team demonstrated the values. This should be both positive and constructive feedback that the team can work on for the next meeting. When team members know they are being observed, their behaviours change. This reinforces the desired behaviours the team aspires to demonstrate, and becomes habitual.

Schedule check-ins: Facilitate quarterly meaningful conversations about how you are demonstrating your values outside of meetings in your day-to-day. It is a great way to give positive feedback to your peers and share stories. Collectively reflect on your team's purpose in moments that matter. Over time, gather feedback from key internal and external stakeholders outside the team.

Review regularly: Teams are not static. Its purpose is not a fixed endpoint, it continuously adapts and evolves, and will guide conversations, decisions, and actions that the team takes over time. Encourage ongoing dialogue to realign and redefine the team's purpose and values collaboratively. Challenges, context, external factors, people, and behavioural expectations will influence both. At least annually, review the team's purpose and values to see if they still fit.

By making purpose and values a living part of the team's culture, they become a powerful tool for alignment, engagement, and long-term success.

CHAPTER 3

Meaningful Work

If you're going to live, leave a legacy.
Make a mark on the world that can't be erased.

— Maya Angelou

Meaning and work

One of our primary needs is a sense of belonging. Working together on meaningful work strengthens relationships and builds bonds and connections beyond just the tasks at hand.

When we find our work meaningful, it tends to align with our personal values, we see the impact it has, and it feels worthwhile. We all subjectively assess the value, impact, and meaning of the work we do. This is usually not at a task level but rather an accumulation of experiences over time. These experiences shape our sense of purpose and create a belief that our work is valuable—to ourselves and to others.

In *Drive: The Surprising Truth About What Motivates Us*, author Dan Pink uncovers the science of motivation. He argues that for simple tasks, extrinsic rewards like money and bonuses motivate us. For complex and creative work, intrinsic motivators that come from within are far more powerful. He suggests that autonomy (the desire to direct our own lives), mastery (the challenge of improving our skills in our field), and purpose (what we do matters) are the core elements of intrinsic motivation. How do you motivate your people with the autonomy, skills, and understanding that their work matters?

In the article 'Making work meaningful from the C-suite to the frontline', McKinsey found that when employees find their work meaningful, their performance increases by 33%, they become 75% more committed to their organisation, and they are 49% less likely to leave. Similarly, KPMG's *Global Customer Experience Excellence Report 2019* found that workers who believe they are having a social impact are twice as satisfied as those who don't.

In *Man's Search for Meaning*, Frankl suggests that we can find meaning in three places: work, love, and courage. Meaning is unique to the individual.

Asking yourself "What is my purpose in life?" can feel overwhelming. In *The Heart of Business*, businessman and former Best Buy CEO Hubert Joly offers words of caution when searching for meaning—don't expect it to simply appear. Meaning is a work in progress. It doesn't have to be a grand, noble act or a mission to save lives; it can be found in small, everyday contributions. Start by focusing on what drives you, what brings you energy, and what brings you joy.

Ikigai means 'reason for being' and focuses on finding value in daily life—it's a journey, not a framework. The word comes from the Japanese *iki* (life) and *gai* (reason). Rather than being solely work-related, *ikigai* is a holistic way of living, embracing the joy of everyday experiences. The well-known ikigai Venn diagram is misattributed. The Venn diagram was actually developed by Andrés Zuzunaga in

2011 as a way to explain purpose. Zuzunaga, an astrologer working with clients on their natal charts, had been contemplating why we were put on this earth. Through his practice of daily meditation, he states that the model came through him. Over six months, he refined the model into the Venn diagram we now recognise. It poses four fundamental questions:

- What do you love?
- What are you good at?
- What does this world need?
- What can you be paid for?

If you want to explore your purpose at work, create four columns with the above headings. Write down everything that comes to mind. Then, highlight areas where there is overlap—these are the areas where you may want to focus more energy and attention.

Australian recruiting firm Beaumont People's *2023 Meaningful Work Insights Report*, which surveyed 4,000 Australian employees, found a significant shift in what people find meaningful about work since the COVID-19 pandemic. The top three contributors to meaningful work were:

1. **Safety:** 70% of employees said they would leave an organisation if they didn't feel physically, mentally, or emotionally safe (a 10% increase from pre-pandemic levels).
2. **Teamwork:** 63% strongly agreed that contributing to team goals was a motivating factor (up from 42%).
3. **Purpose:** 58% expressed a strong desire to make a societal impact (up from 52%).

This study was the first Australian research to integrate psychological and sociological factors, analysing meaningful work at an individual, job, organisational, and societal level.

Connecting people to the impact of their work

For some people, finding meaning at work is easy—those in health-care, environmental work, or social impact roles can clearly see the difference they make. But for others, particularly in roles where the impact isn't immediately visible, it requires more intentional effort. This is where understanding motivation comes in.

🌐 REAL-WORLD CASE STUDY

Thriving at Hive—Find out what drives your people

Hive Legal have individual conversations about what motivates each of their people. They don't assume everyone is the same. Team members will engage with the organisation's purpose from different angles.

Melissa Lyon shared, *"We embrace diversity within the team; we're all motivated in different ways. Everyone brings different skills, contributions, and approaches to the team. You need to find ways that are broad enough to keep people feeling engaged, motivated, and fulfilled with what they are doing."*

Joanna Green added, *"We offer a lot of flexibility in our team. There's a real mix of work and a variety of clients, so people have the opportunity to specialise based on what energises them. We talk about this pretty early on—through 'Thrive at Hive', our career growth program, and in ongoing conversations—asking: What kind of work do you love? What gets you out of bed in the morning?*

For some people, it's about the clients—it's more about human connection than the technical task. For others, it's about variety. And then there are those who prefer a deep focus on one thing. There's room for all of that, even within one team. Over time, we support people to settle into an area that really fits.

We regularly check in with the team about this—what sparks that sense of purpose? What makes you feel like you're making a difference? We encourage this kind of reflection, because meaningful work looks different for everyone."

Hive Legal have authentic conversations to understand their people deeply. There's genuine flexibility to specialise by client or matter type, and room for variety or deep focus within the same team.

Meaningful work looks different for everyone.

What truly drives someone? What do they value? When we tap into this, it becomes easier to help them connect their work to a greater purpose.

Your role as the leader is to help people see and feel the value of their contributions. It is the leader's role to make the connection for an individual to the four levels of purpose: organisational purpose, team purpose, meaningful work, and personal values.

You can inspire performance by linking personal values to meaningful work, in the following ways:

- **Understand your people:** Get to know their personal values, aspirations, and motivations. Recognise that these will be different for each person in your team, and likely from your own. Everyone is unique.
- **Connect daily work to meaning:** Help individuals see how their contributions align with their values, the team's purpose, and the organisation's purpose.
- **Communicate the 'why' first:** When assigning work, start with why it matters before diving into what needs to be done and how (consider Simon Sinek's *Golden Circle* approach).

- **Share impact:** After work is completed, highlight the impact it had on team or organisational goals.

What many fail to recognise is that meaningful work can have unintended consequences or downsides. When people feel deeply connected to their work, they may overcommit, take on too much, or sacrifice personal wellbeing in pursuit of impact. It's important to create an environment where meaningful work is balanced with sustainable ways of working.

Meaningful work isn't something leaders can *give* to employees—it's something individuals must discover for themselves. Your role as a leader is to create the conditions where people can find their own sense of purpose, feel connected to their contributions, and see the impact of what they do every day. This helps to unlock potential in team members and ultimately helps them thrive.

Purposeful roles

Every member of the team wants to feel like they are adding value. Roles and responsibilities need to be clearly articulated, especially when accountabilities shift or there is an overlap. When it is not clear, it causes confusion, ambiguity, and often tension between team members. If not acknowledged, this can lead to politics or duplication of work, further reinforcing silos within teams. Thriving teams need role clarity, which leads to clearer expectations and accountability, less stress, and fewer disagreements.

Role clarity significantly lifts the engagement of team members. According to Gallup, the most fundamental engagement element is knowing what is expected of you. Globally, only 45% of employees know what is expected of them at work, a decline of 11% since March 2020. Why is this number so low? It is likely related to restructuring, additional expectations, job responsibilities, and hybrid teams.

Every team member brings unique strengths. We want to leverage these strengths with complementary skill sets. When I work with teams and I ask them what their team's strengths are, nearly every team acknowledges the knowledge, skills, and abilities of their peers. This shows that they value, respect, and appreciate other team members' capabilities. A great starting point is getting team members to share their skills, experience, and backgrounds. This helps team members get to know each other and not assume that they are defined by their current role. A lot of people have diverse backgrounds, and we can wrongly assume based on the role title what someone's past experiences may have been.

Each team member must be clear on their roles and responsibilities, as well as their teammates'. This should be documented in a meaningful job description. This provides clarity for individuals, reduces duplication, and avoids ambiguity. Often within teams, we need to clearly articulate and be transparent about who is leading or working on certain priorities. Use your meetings to create this visibility and transparency.

⊕ REAL-WORLD CASE STUDY

No queen bee in the Hive

Hive Legal have deliberately avoided a Managing Partner model. Each Principal is a director-shareholder managing a clearly defined area of the business, alongside their own practice, supported by a small operations team. The leadership team has worked together for a decade or more, so trust is high. They understand each other's strengths and play to them.

Principal Joanna Green said, *"We have developed a management model that builds on everyone's strengths. We have a flat structure and work with strong relationships. We make decisions collaboratively. This is different to traditional models, which focus on billable targets and ignore their non-billable contributions, such as developing others. This limits collaboration. We trust that everyone is aligned and pulling towards our common purpose, and we are aligned on this."*

Each member of the Hive leadership team knows what they are responsible for, and what's expected of them. They play to their strengths and have clarity and ownership. Like bees in the hive, everyone understands the purpose of their role and how it enables Hive's shared purpose and vision.

The right people in the right roles

As leadership expert and author of *Good to Great*, Jim Collins says get the right people on the bus and in the right seats. Be intentional about the people who make up the team. This shapes the team's dynamics, how decisions are made, how conflict is navigated, and how people stretch each other. Teams benefit from diverse perspectives across age, gender, cultural background, neurodiversity, technical expertise, and life experience. The reason this matters is simple: diverse teams see more, spot risks earlier, and generate better solutions.

In *The Diary of a CEO* podcast, Steven Bartlett talks about how he spends over a third of his time recruiting—because he knows how critical the right people are. It's a reminder that building a high-performing team is not something we squeeze in between meetings. It's core business. Hire slow and fire fast. Prioritise hiring the right people, considering the cultural fit and impact on your team's dynamics.

Teams benefit from diverse backgrounds, experiences, and technical strengths. This seems to be the most consistent thing that members of a team praise; individuals within teams tend to value the skills, capabilities, and expertise of their team. Especially when different from their own. Make sure you invest time in getting the right people on the team, with complementary skillsets.

Leaving a legacy

Helping individuals establish a purpose that transcends the here and now allows their contribution to extend beyond themselves, creating an enduring impact. Especially for team members who have been in the organisation for a long time, are mature-aged, or are acutely purpose-driven. Spend time unpacking the legacy you want to leave as a team.

An insurance company leadership team I work with has 241 years of service at the organisation among the 11 team members. We have focused on their team purpose and the legacy they want to leave. This is what we did.

Start by reflecting individually:

- What is your legacy?
- Are you living your legacy?

Then share these reflections collectively to uncover the deeper purpose that sits beneath the surface for each individual.

As a team, explore questions like:

- What legacy do we want to leave on this organisation?
- What impact do we want to have on the world?

- To achieve this legacy, what do we need to think, feel, or do differently?
- What's holding us back?

Try this with your team.

🌐 REAL-WORLD CASE STUDY

The Matildas leaving a legacy

In 2023, Australia stopped to watch the Matildas' nail-biting penalty shootout against France in the FIFA Women's World Cup—a win that saw them reach the semi-finals for the first time in history. But what made this team remarkable wasn't just their performance on the field. It was the clarity of purpose that fuelled them.

Coach Tony Gustavsson spoke often about their collective purpose: *to inspire the nation, leave a lasting legacy, and create real change in women's sport.* They weren't just playing for trophies—they were playing for impact.

The team had built deep trust, with strong relationships and a culture that valued each of their skills and strengths. You could see it during the shootout, with extra time featuring critical saves by goalkeeper Mackenzie Arnold. The shootout was the longest in World Cup history, with 20 penalty kicks before Cortnee Vine kicked the winning goal. Her first-ever penalty made history for the Matildas. The entire game showed the belief they had in each other.

Despite the presence of big names like Sam Kerr, the Matildas operated as a team first—putting shared goals ahead of individual recognition. Even Kerr herself spent time on the bench to give others space to step up. What the Matildas showed us was teamwork after 10 penalties each, winning 7–6.

Their purpose wasn't just about winning games. It was about elevating the sport, inspiring girls across the country, and building something that would outlast them. In doing so, they created a burning platform for change—not just in soccer, but in the visibility and value of women's sport in Australia.

The Matildas didn't just play for now. They played for the future. And that's what legacy looks like.

Purpose

Purpose is the foundation of a thriving team. It brings meaning to work, aligns individuals to a shared vision, and fuels engagement, motivation, and performance. A strong team purpose isn't just a statement—it's something that is actively lived and embedded in daily work, decision-making, and team culture.

A thriving team doesn't just *have* a purpose—it *lives* it. When a team is connected to a shared purpose, collaboration improves, silos break down, and decision-making becomes clearer. Without it, teams risk becoming fragmented, with individuals operating in isolation.

Leaders play a crucial role in helping team members connect to the meaning of their work, ensuring they see how their contributions align with the organisation's broader goals. Purpose-driven teams are more resilient, adaptable, and ultimately more successful. But purpose isn't static—it evolves as the team grows, faces challenges, and redefines its direction over time.

A team purpose isn't something that can be imposed—it's something that teams must discover, shape, and integrate into their culture. As a leader, your role is to create the right conditions for purpose to thrive, ensuring it becomes more than just words—it becomes the driving force behind everything your team does. Connect meaning to the work your team does. When teams truly connect with their purpose and work, they don't just function—they *thrive*.

What thriving teams do differently:

- Have a meaningful team purpose that unites the team.
- Have team values that drive their behaviour and that they bring to life each day.
- Are connected to the impact of their work.

Actions

1. **Clarify and align on purpose.** Ensure the team has a clear, shared purpose that resonates with everyone and aligns with organisational goals. Regularly revisit and refine it as circumstances evolve.

2. **Make purpose visible in daily work.** Integrate purpose into meetings, decisions, and conversations. Display it in shared spaces—meeting rooms, workspaces, agendas, or collaboration tools. Start meetings with an example of how the team has lived its purpose that week.

3. **Connect work to meaningful impact.** Frame tasks in terms of impact, not just output—starting with *why* before *what* and *how*. Close the feedback loop by sharing how completed work contributes to team and organisational success.

4. **Strengthen team cohesion through values.** Co-create a set of team values that reinforce purpose, define behaviours that bring those values to life, and foster an environment where accountability and psychological safety thrive.

5. **Encourage peer accountability of your purpose and values.** Rotate the role of meeting chair, assign a rotating *observer* to reflect on values in action, and embed peer recognition into team rituals to reinforce purpose-driven behaviours.

RESOURCES

www.thrivingculture.com.au/ttbook

PART 2

Relationships

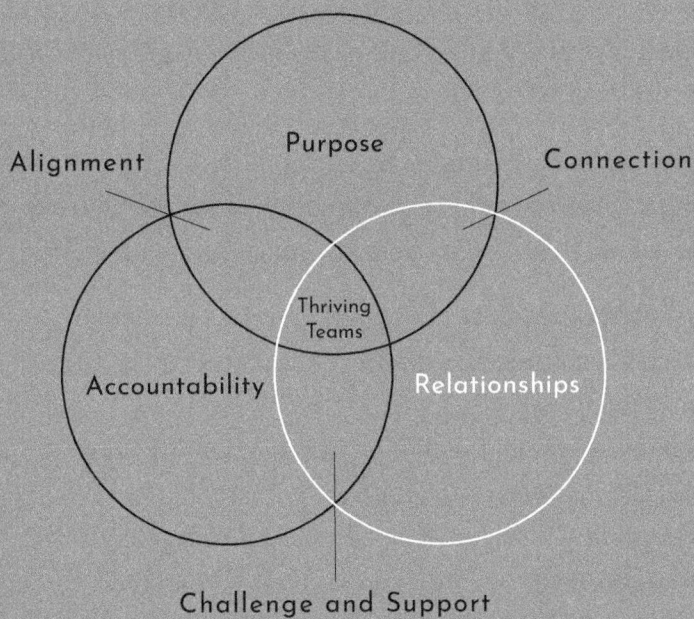

Alignment

Purpose

Connection

Thriving
Teams

Accountability

Relationships

Challenge and Support

In our everyday lives, positive relationships make us feel connected and give us a sense of belonging—a core human need. One of the longest-running longitudinal studies of human life, now over 85 years old, found that relationships are the single most important factor for happiness, health, and longevity (Waldinger & Schulz, 2023). The relationships we build at work are a big part of this picture, shaping not only our wellbeing but also how well our teams thrive. Thriving teams are built on strong relationships, shaping how we interact and work together. Nearly all research on team effectiveness highlights the importance of relationship quality, reinforcing the need to build professional and effective connections within the team. This doesn't mean team members need to be friends or even like each other—it means cultivating healthy, respectful interactions that build collaboration and trust—enabling productive relationships.

Thriving teams demonstrate care and compassion for one another as individuals and as a collective. When we think about relationships at work and in teams, some fundamental areas are most important:

- **Psychological safety:** The belief that it is safe to take interpersonal risks in a group, without fear of negative consequences.
- **Trust:** The strength of one-on-one relationships and reliability between individuals.
- **Belonging:** The sense of being valued and accepted within the team.

When we have strong relationships, team members get to know each other beyond work and also lean into difficult conversations when needed, have healthy debates, and have each other's backs. This is why Relationships intersect with Connection and Challenge and Support in the Thriving Teams Model.

Gallup's *Q12 Meta-Analysis* paints a slightly different picture. As Claire DeCarteret, Managing Director for APAC at Gallup, said on the *Thriving Leaders Podcast*: "Having a best friend at work is a controversial question as it is extreme language. However, it's demonstrably linked to safety—psychosocial safety, psychological safety, and physical safety. If you've got a best friend at work, someone who cares about you, you're more likely to show up, so there is less attrition and team members have each other's backs." This matters less for Executives. Now I'm not suggesting that we need to force friendships, but relationships matter, especially in high-performing teams.

🌐 REAL-WORLD CASE STUDY

Why strong relationships are the glue at Insync

Insync is a purpose-led consultancy that helps organisations improve performance through insight-driven strategy and meaningful employee engagement. Known for their high-trust, high-care culture, Insync partners with clients across private, public, and community sectors to improve alignment, engagement, and governance. Their team of researchers, analysts, psychologists, and facilitators work across everything from employee experience to deliberative community engagement. With a strong belief in practising what they preach, Insync has consistently achieved top decile results in both engagement and alignment—and a 100% trust rating from their own employees. Jeremy Summers, CEO of Insync, shared on the *Thriving Leaders Podcast* that leading a thriving team in a remote-first world takes intentionality.

"Our secret sauce is our people. Strong relationships at Insync aren't left to chance—we work at them. There's no internal competition here. We're all in it together, and we've built a culture where people feel safe to speak up.

We've got a set of clearly stated values at Insync—forward thinking, partnership, accountability, truth, and a high-performance attitude—but we also have a set of unspoken values that are just as important. Things like kindness, togetherness, support, having fun, and a sense of humour. You won't see them written anywhere, but everyone knows that's who we are. Even if they don't before they join, they'll work it out pretty quickly."

Strong relationships anchored in trust and psychological safety are underpinned by lived values at Insync.

We build relationships with others when we have a genuine interest in them and in what they are saying. This requires three fundamental skills, which we will unpack in Chapter 10 – Healthy Debate. They are listening to learn, asking curious questions, and sharing perspectives.

We will explore relationships in thriving teams by unpacking psychological safety and trust in this part of the book.

CHAPTER 4

Psychological Safety

Psychological safety is the way
you get the work done and achieve
your most challenging goals.

— Amy Edmondson, on the *Thriving Leaders Podcast*

In the mid-1990s, Amy Edmondson was completing her PhD research on the relationship between errors and teamwork in hospitals. She hypothesised that lower-performing teams would report more mistakes while higher-performing teams would report fewer. Makes sense. She was stoked when the data came back showing a statistically significant correlation—until it shifted to shock: the results actually showed the opposite. The highest-performing teams reported mistakes 10 times more often than the lower-performing teams.

This accidental discovery led Edmondson to a new conclusion: the best teams didn't necessarily make more mistakes, but they were more willing to report them. To test her new hypothesis, she conducted a blind study to remove bias, with a research assistant who was not aware of her hypothesis or the previous findings. Through observations and interviews, the research assistant found that high-performing teams felt comfortable speaking up, admitting mistakes, and openly working to prevent future errors. In contrast, lower-performing teams tended to hide or mask mistakes due to fear of negative consequences.

Edmondson went on to publish a landmark paper in 1999, which introduced the term 'psychological safety', fundamentally shifting how we think about teams, performance, and learning in the workplace.

Psychological safety gained wider attention in 2016 when Charles Duhigg, author of *The Power of Habit*, wrote an article for *The New York Times Magazine* about Google's Project Aristotle. Google found that psychological safety was the most important factor in a high-performing team. This revelation brought the concept into mainstream conversations about team effectiveness.

At its core, psychological safety is the environment in which people can take interpersonal risks in a group. It's a shared belief among team members about how others will respond if someone admits a mistake, asks for help, seeks feedback, or proposes a bold idea. Teams with high psychological safety don't fear punishment or humiliation when speaking up with concerns or challenges. Amy Edmondson shared on the *Thriving Leaders Podcast*, "These learning behaviours don't have a certain guaranteed result, but individuals feel okay to take those risks as they won't be harmed for doing so."

Psychological safety is crucial for creating a work environment where team members feel comfortable taking these risks without fear of negative consequences. It allows individuals to speak openly, address difficult issues, and manage conflicts effectively. Team members are not punished or humiliated for sharing ideas, questions, concerns, or mistakes. This leads to a culture where mistakes are seen as opportunities for learning, and diversity of thought is appreciated, leading to more innovation and high performance.

In several of Edmondson's subsequent studies, teams with high psychological safety were more open, able to navigate conflict effectively, and better at learning from mistakes. Without fear acting as a barrier, they were also more innovative, embraced diverse perspectives, and took more calculated risks.

Teams that feel safe to speak up, share ideas, and ask for help without fear of judgement are more engaged, creative, and productive. When team members feel supported, they can focus on doing their best work rather than being weighed down by stress, uncertainty, or workplace tension. This not only improves team retention and performance but also strengthens overall team culture and outcomes.

There is a false assumption that psychological safety is easy. It's not. According to McKinsey, only 26% of leaders consistently demonstrate behaviours that contribute to psychological safety within teams, despite 89% of employees believing that psychological safety is essential. It can be challenging to maintain, and it needs to be felt by the entire team for it to truly exist.

A common misconception is that psychological safety is about being nice. Psychological safety is actually about having tough conversations, disagreeing, debating, and sharing diverse perspectives and ideas. Polite and passive cultures do not innovate or outperform.

TEAM IN PRACTICE

The 'Nice' Team

In a mid-sized not-for-profit, the leadership team was made up of passionate people deeply committed to the cause. They valued harmony and were highly respectful of one another, but their politeness often got in the way of progress. Team meetings were friendly and pleasant, but the tougher issues were avoided.

Conflict was seen as destructive rather than constructive, so the group rarely debated ideas. This meant that decision-making dragged on, with issues being revisited multiple times but never resolved. Opportunities to improve services and innovate were often missed.

The CEO recognised the team's reluctance to lean into discomfort and was frustrated by the lack of robust dialogue. As they put it:

- "We're nice to each other, but we're not honest enough."
- "It feels like we're walking on eggshells instead of saying what needs to be said."
- "Decisions keep circling because no one wants to disagree."

They united around their shared goal, 'to create financial sustainability by diversifying funding streams'. They had an open conversation about what this required of them in terms of their leadership and interactions with each other. They developed team values and were explicit about the behaviours they expected of each other. This included:

- Be open to feedback and give feedback readily.
- Share your perspective and be honest.
- Encourage healthy debate.

They rotated the chair of the meeting and had a meeting observer. With support, the team learnt how to have constructive conflict by building psychological safety and normalising debate. Meetings became sharper, with time dedicated to testing ideas and addressing concerns openly. This shift not only sped up decision-making but also helped the organisation innovate in how it delivered on its strategy.

Difference between psychosocial safety and psychological safety

There is some confusion regarding the difference between psychological safety and psychosocial safety in the workplace. While both concepts are equally important from a leadership, health, and wellbeing perspective, they refer to different aspects. Leaders must understand the differences between the two, especially in the context of recent legislation changes in Australia around employer obligations.

Psychological safety focuses on interpersonal relationships, communication, and culture, allowing people to be open and vulnerable.

Psychosocial safety, on the other hand, refers to the policies, practices, and procedures organisations implement to ensure their employees' psychological health and safety. It relates to safeguarding employees' mental health by managing psychosocial risks and hazards in the workplace. This often involves addressing the work environment for factors such as excessive workload, workplace bullying, role ambiguity, interpersonal conflicts, job insecurity, poorly managed change, and a lack of job control. Not acting on it can lead to stress, burnout, and mental health impacts.

The focus is on policies, practices, and structures that influence the psychological wellbeing of employees.

As a leader, you have a responsibility for psychological safety within your team but also to actively manage psychosocial risks. Supporting employees' wellbeing goes beyond encouraging open communication—it requires taking action to remove systemic barriers that cause distress and disengagement. This can include:

- Role design and clarity on who is accountable and responsible.

- Helping team members prioritise tasks to avoid overwhelm.
- Checking in regularly to assess workload and emotional wellbeing.
- Addressing any workplace conflicts or tensions proactively.
- Setting clear expectations so there is minimal ambiguity about what is expected.
- Managing change and communications effectively.
- Streamlining processes and reducing complexity in the system.
- Modelling healthy work-life balance to create a supportive culture.
- Having clear policies around bullying, harassment, and discrimination, and making it safe and clear for employees about how to report these without fear of retribution.

By understanding both psychological and psychosocial safety, leaders can create a work environment where people feel safe, supported, and empowered to do their best work.

Psychological safety within teams

There are many factors that influence psychological safety within a team. Team members can have very different experiences of psychological safety within the same team, and there are plenty of reasons why.

Tenure and familiarity

Tenure is the length of time people have worked together as a team. When you're new to a team, you might not know the unspoken norms or how open people are to sharing and challenging ideas. This can make you more cautious about speaking up. Some research suggests a curvilinear relationship with tenure and psychological safety.

For teams that are newly formed, there is a sense of excitement about the new role or team, and people have an eagerness to contribute. Established teams have built deep relationships founded on trust and shared identity, and tend to have higher psychological safety. After a year, psychological safety lowers. This may be attributed to team members holding back as they don't have the answers, avoiding conflict, feeling pressure to conform, or based on the feedback they receive when they have spoken up in the past (Keepmann et al., 2016; Blanding, 2024).

Familiarity is how well the team knows each other's strengths, weaknesses, experiences, and personality style that influences their behaviours. The more familiar the team is with each other, the safer they feel when communicating and engaging. (See Chapter 8 – Togetherness)

Past experiences

If someone has been shut down or felt undermined in previous teams, they'll often arrive with their guard up and may be more risk-averse. But good experiences can be carried over too, boosting confidence from the get-go. If you've seen positive outcomes from taking risks in previous roles, you're more likely to feel confident doing it again.

Acknowledging past experiences can be useful, especially if you are noticing a team member is holding on to the past or bringing baggage. Or if a new team member seems apprehensive to share their ideas or challenge, ask questions to understand their past experiences. Helping and supporting them to get closure on the past so they can move forward is important. Likewise, for a team that has unhelpful baggage, addressing this collectively so they can move forward together is important.

Competition

Some team members have greater access to information, which naturally gives them more power. Add in status differences—like role, title, or years of experience—and each person's sense of safety can shift dramatically.

To alleviate this, leaders should be conscious to be transparent and share relevant information equally so that team members are on the same page. Even rotating the meeting chair can help shift status slightly within a team's dynamics.

Competition can be healthy. It is the classic push that inspires everyone to excel. Other times it's unhealthy, more about egos or looking good than it is about the greater good of the team. When people worry that their credibility or status is on the line, they tend to hold back.

Psychological safety and diversity

Understanding and valuing our similarities and differences is one of the first places to start with a team. We are all uniquely different; that's what makes this world an interesting place.

Personality style

We all have natural personality styles that influence how we behave. Getting to understand your teammate's personality style helps with communication, idea generation, decision-making, implementation, and working together. Personality profiles give a common language to discuss behaviour as a team. This helps us fast-track our relationships so we can leverage each other's strengths. (See Chapter 8 – Togetherness)

Extroverted people are more likely to share their thoughts quickly and vocally, while introverted team members will want time to reflect. One of my key reflections as a facilitator is not assuming that just because someone is silent, they are not doing the work. People process things differently and need time to reflect before forming a view. Team members' comfort levels with confrontation will also influence how likely they are to speak up or challenge others' perspectives. The good thing is that this is a skill that can be developed, even if you feel discomfort doing this in the moment.

Cultural differences

Psychological safety is a universal phenomenon. However, there are differences across cultures. Asian cultures often exhibit high power distance. This means that hierarchy is important; team members are less likely to challenge authority or speak up. Noting that Asia is a broad, diverse region, these observations are general and don't factor in the nuances between countries in Asia, which vary greatly. Lower power distance cultures, such as Nordic countries, are known to demonstrate higher psychological safety due to egalitarian norms (Anker, 2023). Countries such as Japan and India have collectivist cultures; their focus is on group cohesion, which is great for collaboration, but inhibits individual expression and limits diverse viewpoints. Individualistic cultures such as the United States and Australia are encouraged to express their opinions and ideas. However, there is a risk of overconfidence, a lack of diverse perspectives, and systemic biases (Anker, 2023).

According to Hofstede Insights' in 'Country comparison: Australia', Australia ranks as the second highest individualistic culture globally, second only to the United States. People tend to prioritise their individual goals over the collective. Australia has a low power distance score which supports an egalitarian society, meaning that hierarchy and communication is less formal and more participative (UK Essays, 2024). This is despite Australia being one of the most multicultural countries in the world.

When teams operate across cultures, such as in multinationals or borderless companies, these differences need to be factored in and discussed as a group. This way, we can understand and value our similarities and differences. Teams will tend to conform to where the majority of team members sit culturally. It's important to note the impact these cultural dynamics have on the environment and, therefore, psychological safety within the team. This should not be seen as a barrier, but rather as an opportunity for learning and adapting. Have open discussions about cultural norms and communication styles so that situations don't get misinterpreted.

A study of 265 Australian workers conducted by Deakin University found that focusing on our differences and diversity causes anxiety and can lead to a reduction in knowledge sharing. This is why we need to understand both our similarities and our differences.

Factors such as tenure, familiarity, past experiences, status, power dynamics, competition, personality styles, cultural differences, and neurodiversity all shape how willing each person is to take risks or challenge the status quo. That then influences whether people perceive their team as psychologically safe. This is why you can often end up with a mixed bag of perceptions within the same team. Recognising these differences—and discussing them openly—goes a long way towards building a culture of psychological safety and innovation.

The leader's role in cultivating psychological safety

Everyone in the team influences the psychological safety. The leader has a disproportionate influence on psychological safety within the team because they set the tone. The reality is that if your team isn't feeling psychologically safe, they are unlikely to tell you. Team members will remain silent if they feel that if they speak up, it will be dismissed.

Leaders play a critical role. A 2023 MIT study found that when leaders personally connect with teams and encourage people to speak about what matters to them, psychological safety levels rise.

Yes, the leader of a team has *authority*—but to be effective, they also need *influence*.

When the leader doesn't feel psychologically safe

There are instances where it can feel like the team vs the leader. This is a dysfunctional place to be, but very common. As a result, the leader might withdraw.

A leadership role gives you formal authority. You have permission to speak and be heard. Your role title does not necessarily give you influence though. When a leader feels like they are not psychologically safe, there can be other psychosocial issues at play, such as upward bullying. Don't confuse discomfort with a lack of psychological safety. When we are challenged, it feels uncomfortable, but that doesn't mean it is unsafe.

Amy Edmondson recommended in the *Thriving Leaders Podcast* to make this a discussable topic as a team. She suggested asking questions like: "What I'm noticing is when I say or do this, the response I get is that. What are you experiencing? My intent is ..."

Edmondson explained, "This takes vulnerability and courage to put the unsaid into the arena. But it is likely to give you information that you may not have, so collectively you can work through this challenge together. This becomes the object of learning. It is an essential conversation to have because the status quo is not working. If this feels out of reach or unrealistic for some leaders, get a facilitator or coach present to lead that conversation."

What to do when the leader is the problem

Let's say you're on the team and the leader's behaviour is creating an unsafe environment. What do you do?

Model good behaviours: Model the behaviours you expect, and encourage other team members to do this also, to see if this shifts the team climate. Team members can collectively influence the team culture by demonstrating open communication and support from each other. This can help to influence the behaviours of others.

Give feedback if you can: Yes, it can feel like a career-limiting move. But if done thoughtfully, it might enlighten the leader to something they don't realise they're doing. Focus on how the environment limits the team's ability to hit goals (e.g. impacting creativity, blocking diverse viewpoints). If direct feedback is too daunting, suggest an anonymous approach—like a Thriving Teams Diagnostic—to bring attention to safety issues without singling anyone out.

Seek support: Share this challenge with other trusted people who could influence the situation. This could be speaking with their leader, peers, or Human Resources. Do this in a constructive way that supports the leader through feedback, coaching, or training.

Rather than finger-pointing, the team should work collectively for positive change within the team.

How to build psychological safety with your team

As a leader, it can be tricky to know if your team truly feels safe, because the more unsafe they are, the less likely they'll be to admit it.

Leaders do indeed shape psychological safety, but the magic is that *everyone* can influence it. If you're the leader, remember that feeling safe doesn't always mean feeling *comfortable*. A little bit of discomfort can mean healthy stretch and growth. Your job is to observe and evaluate, create the right environment, and read between the lines. Open up, check in, and if the team vibe is off, don't be afraid to call it out. Communication is key and don't feel like you need to do it alone.

Psychological safety isn't a tick-box exercise—it's an ongoing focus because the team's climate can change in a heartbeat. People come and go, goals shift, and different values or belief systems can pop up. That means psychological safety needs constant nurturing.

⊕ REAL-WORLD CASE STUDY

Unconditional positive regard

The Australian Financial Complaints Authority (AFCA) exists to resolve some of the most complex and emotionally charged disputes in the financial sector. Over the last six years, the workforce has tripled in size to meet the demands, especially in scam-related issues, financial hardship, and banking and finance complaints. It's high-pressure work, and yet AFCA consistently ranks as one of the best places to work in Australia, with extremely high employee engagement results.

On the *Thriving Leaders Podcast*, Greg Pickering, Senior Manager of Insurance, shared what's behind that reputation.

Greg said the AFCA approach is grounded in fairness, transparency, and accessibility. It aims to create conditions where people can speak honestly without fear of retribution. In his team he calls this "unconditional positive regard"—the idea that, no matter what happens, team members continue to view each other positively while challenging assumptions and stretching each other's thinking.

As Greg said, *"We are emotional creatures. Things can affect us deeply and personally. When we express those things, sometimes it's almost impossible to remove the emotion. And sometimes it's actually way more beneficial—it's cathartic.*

I need that safety too. And what that means is sometimes when you raise things, my response may feel direct—but it will always be honest. I will always tell you as much as I possibly can. I'll highlight when there's stuff I can't share—and I'll give you the high-level thinking behind it."

Being this explicit with the team so they know what to expect lays the foundations for the team to follow.

Here are some strategies that you may wish to adopt to encourage psychological safety within your team.

Team purpose and a clear direction

Directly asking about psychological safety within the team can be counterproductive. If the team doesn't feel safe, they probably won't tell you. Instead, leaders should focus on the team's purpose, and a clear direction that unites the team around common goals.

Amy Edmondson shared in the *Thriving Leaders Podcast*, "Don't talk about psychological safety. Talk about this incredibly challenging, important work we're trying to do and what it will require of us. Psychological safety is not the goal for a management team. It's a means to the goal."

Firstly, the team needs to be clear on the goal or challenge they are solving. Set the stage. Co-create mutually desirable outcomes. To do this, emphasise the importance of the behaviours you expect to achieve your goals. This could include healthy, challenging debate, a sense of curiosity, an openness to listen, and taking risks. Research shows that linking to a higher purpose increases the likelihood of speaking up if there is a link to something greater than themselves (Blanding, 2024).

Discuss with the team:

- Why are we here? (See Chapter 2 – Team Purpose)
- What must we achieve? (See Chapter 6 – Clear Direction)
- How do we need to interact to get there? (See Chapter 2 – Team Purpose)

Listen, be curious, and speak up

We've all heard the saying, "If you don't have anything nice to say, don't say anything at all." Real conversations don't happen by chance. They occur in environments where people feel safe speaking up without fear of judgement or repercussions. As leaders, it's our responsibility to create that environment. Speaking up and being humiliated is not easy. When a team has psychological safety, it can lead to conversations that drive innovation, push boundaries, and challenge habitual thinking. When people feel fearful or unsafe, they will not speak up.

On the *Thriving Leaders Podcast*, Amy Edmondson shared that high-quality conversations are rare because they require skilful communication, which many people haven't been trained for. Leaders should emphasise the importance of these conversations in achieving team goals, focusing on candour, creativity, and mutual support. This involves a healthy mix of sharing ideas, asking quality questions to draw out knowledge, and acknowledging that speaking up, risk taking, and challenging each other's ideas is hard. It can feel uncomfortable. We need to get comfortable with that discomfort, as this is where the learning and magic happens.

Encourage team members to:

- Listen to learn.
- Ask curious questions.
- Share perspectives.

When you want to express some thoughts start questions with prompts like:

- What I'm grappling with is ...
- I wonder if ...
- I'm curious to understand ...

Listen without the need to fix. Sometimes, the best thing we can do is listen. Empathy builds trust, and trust leads to more openness in the future.

Trade blame for curiosity. Instead of finger-pointing you may ask:

- What led us here?
- What could we do differently next time?
- What have we learnt?

Role model vulnerability and humility

If we're not open about our own challenges, how can we expect our teams to be? Sharing your own struggles sets the tone for openness across the team. Psychological safety emphasises shared vulnerability within a team. This shared awareness can make teams more powerful by fostering openness and honesty. A team needs to lean into their shared vulnerability. Individually each member needs to role model vulnerability. Share where you have made mistakes and what you have learnt in the process. Encourage others to share. Let the team know when you don't have the answer. Humility complements vulnerability as it demonstrates the awareness of your own limitations and values the contributions of others. Vulnerability and humility are traits that can be developed through practice and intentional behaviours.

Develop your leadership capability

A 2022 study by the EcSell Institute highlighted the impact of leadership on psychological safety. Employees who rated their leader's skills as a 9 or 10 out of 10 reported an average psychological safety score of 84%. Conversely, when employees rated their leader's skills as 6 or lower, the average psychological safety rating dropped to just 36%, demonstrating a strong correlation between leadership skills and psychological safety. This reinforces the critical role of leadership in creating psychologically safe teams. Develop your leadership capability.

McKinsey's 2021 report *Psychological safety and the critical role of leadership* found that a consultative and supportive leadership style will build a positive team climate; only then can you as the leader challenge to maintain strong psychological safety.

In the *4 Stages of Psychological Safety*, leadership consultant Timothy Clarke outlines the four stages and suggests that each stage represents a level of safety that helps teams shift to high performance. The stages are: inclusion, learning, contribution, and challenging. I believe all these elements need to exist; however, I don't believe it is a linear model as Clarke suggests.

Building psychological safety isn't a one-off action; it's an ongoing commitment to creating environments where people feel supported, valued, and heard. If psychological safety is something you are concerned with, find a team coach to support you and the team to create a high-performing team environment.

CHAPTER 5

Trust

If you want to be trusted. Be trustworthy.

— Stephen R. Covey

The words trust and psychological safety often get used interchangeably. They have subtle differences. Psychological safety is a group norm. It is the experience that the group is having at that moment. Trust is a belief between individuals or entities. In a team, there will be different levels of trust between people, and you will observe different levels of trust between peers. Trust influences your expectations of others. Psychological safety and trust both require a level of vulnerability. You will have a level of trust with the leader in your team. The leader of the team needs to trust the team, so that they can delegate work appropriately and empower people to be accountable.

🌐 **REAL-WORLD CASE STUDY**

Trust is a two-way street at Insync

Insync treats truth as a lived value—it represents trust and psychological safety—and turns it into daily habits. They ritualise clear, regular feedback, rewarding people for raising their hand when things go wrong, and managing by outcomes, not hours. They extend the same trust to their customers too.

On the *Thriving Leaders Podcast*, Jeremy Summers shared how deeply trust and psychological safety are embedded at Insync.

"Truth is one of our values—and it's probably the hardest to live. For me, truth is trust. It's incredibly important for me. The relationships I have with my people—whether they report to me, I report to them, or we're peers—are built on honesty. Sometimes it's tempting not to be 100% honest about something. But we don't allow ourselves that luxury. And it's not just about saying the wrong thing—it's also about not saying the right thing. That kind of silence can be just as damaging. We really encourage our people to speak up. That's how we get better, and it's how we build trust.

Regular, clear feedback is something we live and breathe. Everyone knows what's expected of them, and they know they'll get honest input along the way. One of our stated behaviours is: if you make a mistake, don't worry—put your hand up, we've got your back. That creates a culture where people support each other and don't hide things. It's not about being nice—it's about being kind, and there's a big difference.

Trust is one of those things you can't fake. We're in the top decile for alignment and engagement, but underneath that, what I'm really proud of is that 100% of our people say they trust their leader, 100% say their opinion is valued, and 100% say the ELT (Executive Leadership Team) acts with integrity. That tells me trust isn't just something we talk about—it's real. And trust goes both ways.

We trust our people to do their jobs—and they trust us to have their backs. We trust our people to work where they want, when they want. We focus on outcomes, not hours. We don't micromanage or micro-measure."

Trust isn't a poster at Insync—it's a system, it's who they are. Speak the truth, surface mistakes fast, normalise feedback, and measure what matters.

It's important to understand the neuroscience behind trust. When oxytocin is released in the brain, often referred to as the love hormone, we feel more connected, are more open to others, and our defence mechanisms are lowered. Teams with high levels of trust are 50% more productive (Ross, 2024). It reduces the need to micromanage and improves team members' confidence in their abilities and accountabilities. A McKinsey 2024 study found teams with above-average trust were 3.3 times more efficient and 5.1 times more likely to produce results.

I agree with Patrick Lencioni, that trust is the foundational pillar of a high-performing team. As leaders, we cultivate that trust by showing appropriate vulnerability and building genuine relationships. This isn't about unveiling your deepest, darkest secrets; it's about revealing your human and empathetic side. When team members lack trust, fear starts steering the conversation. People become hesitant to be honest, dodge accountability, and worry that any mistake will be held against them.

In a thriving team, members trust one another on an emotional level. They feel safe acknowledging mistakes or weaknesses because they're confident in their colleagues, the team as a whole, and have everyone's best interests at heart. This is vulnerability-based trust: admitting when you don't have the answer or don't understand something, without worrying about judgement. Teams that trust one another go the extra mile, listen more attentively, and extend forgiveness more readily. Trust is both a choice and a skill that can be developed over time.

High-trust teams make faster decisions, operate more efficiently, and collaborate with ease. Conversely, when trust is low, fear and resistance creep in, raising the risk of communication breakdowns and progress.

Team members have different natural preferences when it comes to trust. Some people, based on their personality, will start from a place of trust. If trust is broken, they will trust again. Others will quietly weigh people up, and give trust and support accordingly. If that trust is broken, it will be withdrawn, and it will be hard to regain. With others, you have to earn trust; it is not a given. Within a team, you will likely have a mix of all of these.

Dr John Gottman, psychologist and relationship researcher, discovered that relationships are far more likely to thrive when there are at least five positive interactions for every negative one. Stephen Covey describes a similar idea in *The 7 Habits of Highly Effective People*, calling it the "emotional trust account". Think of it like a bank account: every positive interaction is a deposit, every negative interaction a withdrawal. When the deposits outweigh the withdrawals, trust grows stronger. If we maintain this ratio, we build and sustain a positive, trusting relationship.

Elements of trust

When the elements of trust align you are on the path to a high-trust environment. In *Trust and Betrayal in the Workplace*, organisational psychologists Dr Dennis Reina and Dr Michelle Reina identify three distinct types of trust—communication, character, and capability. I have adapted their model and added a fourth, consistency, to create the 4Cs—Elements of Trust.

Communication

Trust in communication means sharing knowledge and information transparently, giving and receiving constructive feedback, listening to learn, and speaking truthfully with good intent.

Clear communication creates certainty about where you stand with teammates on shared work and commitments. It is eroded when information is withheld, or gossip and secrecy creep in.

Character

Trust in character centres on integrity and a shared understanding between people. Earned over time, it shows up in behaviours such as delegating appropriately, admitting mistakes, apologising, preserving confidentiality, maintaining boundaries, and showing vulnerability. It relies on being honest about results and expectations and on following through on commitments. It is damaged when this does not occur.

Capability

This is the confidence others place in your competence. It grows when you recognise and acknowledge skills and strengths—both your own and other people's—value their input and help them develop new abilities. Capability trust stretches beyond current expertise; it assumes you will continue to learn. It can be impacted by micromanagement or a lack of feedback on performance.

Consistency

Reacting predictably, so people know what they can expect from you, helps to build trust. This gives people reassurance and ensures 'no surprises'. This is about being reliable and dependable. Be stable in your approach, follow through on promises, and ensure your words match your actions. Consistency means modelling the other Cs—communication, character, and capability—day in, day out. Trust erodes when behaviour becomes inconsistent or unpredictable.

Reflect on the 4Cs in the context of individual relationships within the team. Assess how you are contributing to a trusting relationship and if you may need to focus on an element of the 4Cs.

How to build trust with your team

We're all human—yet in the busyness of work, we don't always take time to connect. People want to feel seen, heard, and valued for more than just what they deliver. Trust takes time, built through shared moments and genuine conversations.

Stephen Covey, in his book *The Speed of Trust*, shares 13 behaviours of high-trust leaders. I have categorised these under the 4Cs so that you can see the behaviours you may need to demonstrate if you need to improve trust in any relationship.

Communication (how you connect):

- talking straight
- creating transparency
- clarifying expectations
- listening first

Character (who you are):

- demonstrating respect
- righting wrongs
- showing loyalty
- confronting reality

Capability (what you can do):

- delivering results
- getting better

Consistency (how reliably you do it):

- practising accountability
- keeping commitments
- extending trust to others

We discuss ways to build trust and connection within your team in Chapter 8 – Togetherness.

Rebuilding trust

It can feel uncomfortable to admit that there is low trust within a team. Trust can be repaired, but it requires focus. In *How to Trust and Be Trusted*, author and Oxford University lecturer Rachel Botsman emphasises that when repairing trust, acknowledge that trust was broken without being defensive, take accountability for actions that led to the breach in trust, take action so it doesn't happen in the future, and then consistently follow through on those commitments made.

In my experience working with leadership teams, it's often about surfacing the underlying issues and sharing these back to the team in a way that gets them talking about the 'elephants in the room'. It can feel uncomfortable, but when the right environment is created, it creates a platform to understand each other's perspective. Ask each team member to reflect on the 4Cs in a relationship with a team member where trust may be broken and assess how the other person may view them. This forces people to consider how they are contributing to the mess, rather than focusing on what the other person is doing wrong. They can then be intentional about what part of the 4Cs they may need to focus on to improve the relationship.

Leaders or other team members often want to facilitate this session. While they may have strong facilitation skills, playing this role can shift team dynamics and impact participation. If possible, engage a team coach or external facilitator so leaders can fully participate as equal team members.

Belonging

We've all experienced that feeling of truly belonging—the sense of community that comes from being part of a tribe. As humans, we crave that connection. Conversely, there are other moments—at work, with friends, or with family—where we've felt like we're on the outer. We feel left out, rejected, or not included, and that leads us to question what we thought we knew. It plants seeds of doubt; we worry, become anxious, fear being rejected, or get caught in competitive behaviours. It also causes a lot of inefficiencies and wasted effort.

⚙ TEAM IN PRACTICE

A founder on the outer

A founder's dream of being acquired by a larger company finally came true. They were relieved to no longer bear the full burden of responsibility and excited by the prospect of scaling their boutique marketing agency with greater resources. With the backing of a bigger organisation, international expansion suddenly looked within reach.

The excitement soon gave way to frustration. While the founder remained on the leadership team, their insights were consistently brushed aside. Leadership meetings became an exercise in tolerance, with condescending nods and polite smiles whenever they shared ideas. The parent company's executives seemed more interested in imposing their way of working than learning the secret sauce that had made the agency valuable in the first place.

The founder described it this way:

- "I feel like a sitting duck—bound by golden handcuffs."
- "They say they value my ideas, but the truth is they ignore them."
- "It's painful watching the company I built start to erode."

They felt disengaged and disempowered, waiting out the required two years for their payout, which was contingent on performance. The risk was real—if the business faltered, so would their financial future. The divide between the founder and the parent company widened, threatening both trust and outcomes.

The turning point came when the founder chose to speak openly with the CEO about how sidelined they were feeling. That honest conversation became a catalyst for change, creating space for both sides to reset expectations. At the same time, the founder recognised the need to adjust their own mindset—shifting from defending "how we've always done it" to being open to the parent company's way of working. By showing some vulnerability and facing into the difficult conversation, they rebuilt trust and found a sense of belonging in the new leadership team. This helped the founder and the business harness the best of both worlds.

Belonging is a fundamental human need. Our brains are hardwired for connection, thanks to the emotional and biological benefits. Research by BetterUp (2019) found that when we feel like we belong in a team, we perform better (a 56% improvement in job performance), are more productive and engaged, and are less likely to chuck a sickie (a 75% decrease) or leave altogether (a 50% reduction in turnover). We feel more motivated and driven. When we feel like we belong, our brain's reward system is activated, releasing dopamine and oxytocin—the 'feel-good' hormones—which enhance motivation, satisfaction, and trust.

People feel they belong when they're valued, can be their authentic selves, are included, and feel trust and psychological safety. As leaders, we need to create the space for that sense of belonging, making sure each team member feels included, valued, and respected.

Leaders also need to demonstrate empathy and compassion for others and use inclusive language. When leaders believe in their team, communicate this and demonstrate actions that support this, it leads to a stronger sense of belonging.

New team members

Teams are always evolving; people come and go, work changes and priorities shift. Especially with the additional complexity of remote and flexible working.

To ensure team success, when you bring new team members in, share the journey that you have been on—challenges and successes. Buddy them up and ensure a robust onboarding process. If there is a strong team culture, they may feel on the outer initially. Which means that it may take longer for them to integrate into the team. Be intentional to bring them into the fold; be open to their ideas and suggestions, rather than closing them down with "we tried that before and it didn't work". Treat them as a valued contributor from the start, and they'll reward you with openness and a willingness to take on more challenges, sooner.

Inclusion

Inclusion means ensuring that every voice is heard, respected, and considered in the team's decision-making. Everyone should feel seen, heard, and valued. Stay open to different communication styles, and set the tone for what is appropriate culturally for your team—not just in your own opinion. Respect diversity of thought and treat people as individuals.

We want every team member to feel welcomed, respected, and valued for their unique perspectives. We want all team members to feel included. There's nothing worse than feeling excluded, and that risk is especially high for new team members who don't yet feel they belong.

Creating an environment that embraces differences, encourages open dialogue, acknowledges biases, and promotes diverse perspectives contributes to a sense of belonging for each individual in the team. They'll bring more of themselves to work, feel they can be genuine, and do their best when they're not wearing a mask to fit in.

Encourage team members to show authenticity, and be the best version of themselves. Demonstrate a genuine interest in others. Show respect and treat people as individuals. Many of us have been taught to 'be professional' but what often happens is we end up being less human as result. Role model vulnerability and transparency in your own behaviour.

Reflect on whether there are behaviours you are demonstrating which are making team members feel excluded. This could be as simple as having a 'go to' team member, which may be perceived as you playing favourites. Be consistent and clear about the precedents you are setting so exchanges feel fair and equal. Educate yourself on any unconscious biases you may hold, and self-reflect regularly.

By creating a culture of inclusion and belonging, you'll find your team members are more engaged, high performing, and ready to step up when challenges arise.

Relationships

Relationships are fundamental to the success of a team. They are the heartbeat that connects us; the healthier the relationships the more that can be achieved. We are hardwired for connection and a sense of belonging. These can be cultivated through building psychological safety and trust within the team. This means that the team can handle challenges, innovate, and achieve great outcomes.

This doesn't mean you need to be mates but there does need to be psychological safety, trust, and a sense of belonging and inclusion for a team to thrive. High-performing teams can show respect and compassion, and still debate and disagree with each other for the greater good of the team. Create the climate and space for team members to speak up and challenge the status quo, all while having each other's backs.

It is often multiple small actions that make the biggest difference.

What thriving teams do differently:

- Create an environment that is psychologically safe.
- Team members build strong individual relationships.
- Have a shared identity and a sense of belonging.

Actions

1. **Create a psychologically safe environment.** Do this by showing curiosity, role modelling taking interpersonal risks, and helping the team develop the skills for high-quality conversations. (See Chapter 10 – Healthy Debate)

Focus on the team's shared goals and what is needed from the team to achieve them. Ask:

- What must we achieve?
- How do we need to work together to get there?

This will inform the expectations and create the environment to do your best work.

2. **Build trust within the team.** Trust comes from what you communicate, who you are, what you can do, and how reliably you do it. Use the 4Cs – Elements of Trust (communication, character, capability, and consistency), to assess relationships with team members. Where trust may have eroded, reflect on which element you may need to focus on to improve the relationship.

3. **Reflect on how you are creating a sense of belonging and inclusion.** In what ways are you making people feel valued, included, and psychologically safe? How are you making sure everyone's voice is heard and respected?

4. **Ensure new starters quickly integrate.** Buddy new team members up with someone with longer tenure. Share the team's purpose and principles. Be open to their views and encourage them to contribute.

5. **Reunite the team.** When a team hits the one-year mark, celebrate this, and find ways to reunite the team to the team purpose and values, and renew goals so that you don't hit the dip in the curve.

RESOURCES

www.thrivingculture.com.au/ttbook

PART 3

Accountability

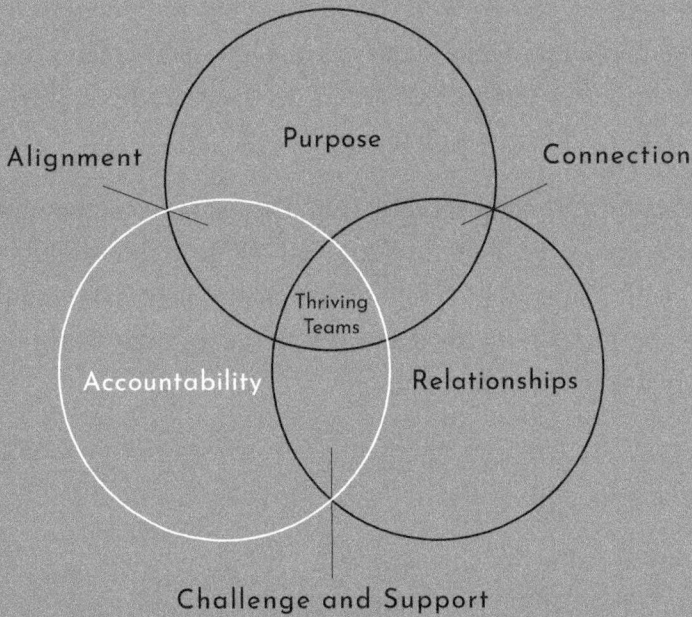

Accountability intersects with Alignment and Challenge and Support in the Thriving Teams Model. Accountability within a team is 'what' you will achieve and by 'when'. This requires a clear direction and mechanisms so that the team can hold each other accountable.

Accountability often gets a bad rap and has become a dirty word in workplaces. People think it's about blame, finger-pointing, justifying mistakes, feeling pressure to perform, or micromanagement. I even heard a new client refer to the 'accountability salute', arms crossed, fingers pointing out, blaming everyone around them.

I am on a mission to change this. Accountability is a privilege. It means someone trusts you to take ownership and get the job done. It should feel empowering that someone has the belief in your skills, knowledge, and experience. Leaders need to shift this negative connotation to a positive one in teams.

Accountability is about clarity. It is delivering on a commitment, using initiative to follow through, and taking responsibility for an outcome. It eliminates ambiguity and creates boundaries and ownership. Accountability involves understanding what is required in terms of quality and timeframes.

Accountability has a heightened focus in organisations. Whether that is because people are:

- Being asked to do more with less.
- Don't feel comfortable holding others accountable.
- Don't have the confidence or skill to give feedback appropriately.
- Don't want to risk upsetting staff out of fear that they may leave.
- Don't want to be perceived as bullying their staff.

Many organisations are experiencing extensive technological and organisational change. With the goal posts shifting, or expectations changing, it becomes even harder to hold others accountable. A culture of accountability is even more important.

Accountability creates clarity, builds trust, and drives results in teams. Teams need to have shared accountability to give them skin in the game.

Before you can focus on accountability, you need to be clear on the direction as a team or organisation. It is nearly impossible to hold people accountable if you don't know what you are holding them accountable to.

In this part of the book we will discuss creating a clear direction and team accountability.

CHAPTER 6

Clear Direction

Without strategy, execution is aimless.
Without execution, strategy is useless.

— Morris Chang

Teams need to be clear on where to focus their energy. Teams need clear direction, whether that is a set of goals, priorities, or a strategy. What I loved in my conversation with Amy Edmondson on the *Thriving Leaders Podcast* was her focus on the work, on the goal as a team. This should be the anchor, as that's what teams are there to do. How they go about doing it then links to relationships, psychological safety, and trust which allows us to do the hard things that teams need to do.

However, teams can find it challenging to make decisions about what is most important. Especially when there are conflicting views or priorities.

Strategy or goal setting is a bit like a hotel buffet. At a buffet, there are a lot of options and food laid out for you. If you charge in without stepping back to look at the bigger picture, you will likely start filling your plate, not aware of the possibilities of what is coming next. You may end up filling your plate too quickly and miss the good stuff.

As a team developing strategy, it is about making deliberate choices of what you are going to put on your plate, resisting the urge to load up. Just because it is in front of you, or your competitor is doing it, doesn't mean you need to add this to your plate. If you've been to a few too many hotel offsites, you'll know the regret of the buffet bellyache. Same goes for teams with no strategic focus—too much on the plate, not enough clear direction, and a lot of indigestion by Q4. The overloaded plate is the equivalent of the overcommitted team. Trying to do everything and not doing anything well. Your team is exhausted as they are burning the candle at both ends. Strategic priorities slip and deadlines aren't hit, which causes trust to erode within the team and beyond.

When you set strategy or goals with your team, it's about:

- Understanding the bigger picture.
- Deciding what to put on your plate.
- Choosing deliberately what you are leaving off.
- Being realistic about when the plate is full.

Strategy

Leadership is about choices. Strategy allows you to make choices of where you will play and where you won't play. This helps inform decision-making and provides guiding principles.

A strategy is a big-picture, long-term view of what you want to achieve as a team. This clarity of direction alleviates ambiguity and confusion about where you are headed. If you are the most senior team in the organisation, you are accountable for setting the strategy for the organisation. Having a clear direction allows all teams to align and understand how they contribute towards the strategy. A strategy articulates what makes your organisation unique, differentiates it, and distinguishes how it provides value. It informs what areas to invest your time and money in, how the organisation should be structured, resourcing requirements, and how you should respond to market and stakeholder needs.

When your team has a clear direction and an understanding of how each person contributes towards it, they are aligned. The more involvement the team has in creating the strategy and setting the goals and plan, the more buy-in they will have to achieve the shared goals. Teams work most effectively when everyone understands, endorses, and commits to shared goals. Clarity ensures everyone understands the decisions, agreements, and direction of the group.

I am not suggesting that every team in the organisation needs its own strategy. It is far better for teams to focus on key goals and how they contribute to the organisational or individual business unit's strategy, so that there is alignment. If teams all go off and create their own strategy, they are often not aligned to the organisational strategy and vision.

How to create a strategy

Firstly, you need to determine who needs to be involved in creating the strategy. Getting the right players in the room and input from key stakeholders is an important first step. Inviting key talent along, or the voice of your customers, can be a useful exercise so that the session isn't so internally focused. This could involve focus group sessions with key stakeholders such as clients, customers, members, boards, or other stakeholders such as your direct reports. Focus groups or listening sessions can provide valuable insight into what's working and what's not.

Pre-work is essential for a successful strategy session. This avoids groupthink by encouraging individual reflection and research ahead of time. Before the session, ask participants to reflect and research individually—this ensures you get all perspectives. You may wish to capture this through an anonymous survey to avoid groupthink in the session.

You need to look internally to review what's been going well—to celebrate and leverage your success—as well as be realistic about what hasn't gone so well. It's important as an organisation to look externally too: what's happening in the industry, market, or geopolitically, as these may impact the organisation or strategy.

I use a SWOT Analysis to do this—exploring the internal (strengths and weaknesses) and the external (opportunities and threats)—and how this information can inform your strategic direction. Alternatively, you may wish to use SOAR (Strengths, Opportunities, Aspirations, and Results), which is a forward-looking, positive approach. However, this can lack an external risk focus.

Here are some example questions you may ask people to consider before a strategy session. You can ask some, or select a couple from each section.

Strengths (internal):

- What are we doing exceptionally well?
- What are our strengths?
- What's our unique selling proposition or competitive advantage?
- What strengths do we see in our people, culture, or ways of working?

Weaknesses (internal):

- Where can we improve?
- What are our weaknesses?
- What systems, processes, resources, capabilities, or technology are lacking?

- What recurring issues or frustrations do we hear from our people, customers, or stakeholders?

Opportunities (external):

- What opportunities exist? (i.e. market, industry, technologies, or strategic partnerships/alliances)
- What are the (emerging) trends in the industry or market?
- What underserved customer needs, services, or products can we address?
- What could we do that no one else is doing?

Threats (external):

- What are our biggest threats? (i.e. market, industry, geopolitical, technologies, regulations, or strategic partnerships)
- What are our competitors doing that we aren't?
- What are our biggest risks to our customers/stakeholders?
- What early warning signs or blind spots may we be ignoring?

Once these have been explored, look for patterns or tensions across quadrants. This can help shape priorities or highlight critical decisions.

What stands out the most from this analysis?

In their book *Playing to Win*, former Procter & Gamble CEO AG Lafley and Roger Martin, former Dean of the Rotman School of Management, set out a practical framework for making the strategic choices that drive business success. They suggest that strategy is a set of hard choices to win in your chosen market, and recommend asking the following five questions:

1. What is our winning aspiration?
2. Where will we play?
3. How will we win?

4. What capabilities must be in place?

5. What management systems are required?

In contrast, motivational speaker Simon Sinek in his book *The Infinite Game* suggests that you don't win, as there is no finish line. You can't tick off strategy and say it is done; it evolves over time and as leaders we need to play a long, infinite game. I believe it is a bit of both. We are aiming to win in the long run, so we need to make decisions that prioritise long-term success over short-term gains—unless, of course, your strategy is to make yourself attractive for acquisition.

To create a strategy, we need to get creative. Creating the right environment to ideate and brainstorm ideas is key. I often like getting people into nature in this phase—it changes the context and environment, enhances creative problem-solving, and improves executive functioning. A walk and talk in green spaces can be so beneficial. It improves energy levels, gets quieter people talking, builds trust, and enhances focus.

When developing strategy, it is important to come together as a team. That's why investing uninterrupted time in offsite sessions is so valuable. The leader should act as a participant and ideally have someone else facilitate the session, so they can focus on listening, engaging, and participating.

Leaders and teams want to walk away from a strategy session with a clear direction.

A 'plan on a page' captures your strategy in a simple, memorable, and digestible way so leaders can communicate and translate it into implementable plans with their team. I recommend you include the following elements in your plan on a page:

- Purpose
- Vision

- Strategic priorities
- Objectives
- Key results
- Values

Purpose is a statement that articulates why the organisation exists. This statement should inspire people and express the change you want to see. Why does the organisation exist?

Vision is where the organisation is headed in the long term (3–10 years). The vision should be aspirational to team members and provide them with a north star. It embeds a unified vision while empowering autonomous teams. Our vision is what we aspire to.

- What are our hopes and dreams by [insert date in the future, i.e. 2030]?
- How will we change the world (audacious dream—so big it feels impossible)?
- What problems are we solving for the greater good?
- Who and what are we aspiring to change?

Where are we today? This is where the SWOT Analysis comes in. If each person attending the strategy session does their own SWOT analysis, then when you can come together you can debate these things, creating one organisational SWOT analysis.

Strategic priorities are the critical areas the organisation will focus on to achieve the vision. Being in business is competitive, and therefore you need to understand what your performance edge is.

- Where will we play?
- How will we get there?
- What do we need to focus on to achieve our vision?
- If it were 5–10 years from now, what needs to have happened?

Leadership and strategy is about making choices. The complexity of the changing and adaptive environment that teams need to operate in means we can't just keep doing more, we need to do differently. We need to stop doing stuff. We need to focus on the most strategic and important things.

Objective and Key Results will be explained shortly.

Values is how you will achieve your strategy. These are the shared beliefs that underpin the culture and anchor to the behaviours you expect of your people.

You may choose to use AI to analyse competitors and stakeholders, understand the external landscape, pull together insights to inform decisions, act as a thought partner, and refine your communication strategy.

🌐 REAL-WORLD CASE STUDY

Clear quad objectives for the Australian Olympic Committee (AOC)

When Matt Carroll stepped into the role of CEO at the Australian Olympic Committee (AOC) in 2017, he wasn't just taking on one of the most prestigious roles in Australian sport; he was going to face one of the most complex Games yet. The Tokyo Olympics during COVID-19.

The AOC Executive Team were clear on expectations and had collective accountability. They created a strategic cycle that matched their culture and the way they operated, in quads. They took time away from the day-to-day, used data, and anchored to their core purpose to ensure they focused on the right things.

Matt said, on the *Thriving Leaders Podcast*:

"We were always really clear: this is what we're here to do, and this is how we're going to do it. The objectives are in black and white—set by the Olympic Charter and our Constitution. We are responsible for getting Australian Olympic teams to Games, including summer, winter, and youth Games. We are also responsible for the promotion of sport in Australia, education, the study of sport, the integrity of sport, and community. You don't get to make them up as you go. So we'd spend a couple of days away from the office, we'd look at what happened the previous quad (four-year cycle), how we performed, and at data.

As an executive team we'd ask: what are the 10 most important things we need to deliver over the next four years? Each person would take ownership of certain objectives, and we'd track them across the quad. But it wasn't just about dividing up a list—it was about owning the purpose. Whether you were the Chief Financial Officer or the Head of Teams, you were just as responsible for delivering on that purpose. That's accountability. You can't be in a role like that and not want to make a difference. And if you don't, then maybe it's time to find something else."

It's important for teams to have a clear direction that is co-created and build a rhythm that fits your context.

To create a thriving strategy, it needs to be implemented. This is often what falls short.

Strategy's a bit like chess. You're not just making moves at the top and hoping the rest of the board follows. You're thinking five steps ahead—anticipating reactions, scenario planning, reading the room, and figuring out how each move sets up the next ones. We can't be certain about outcomes; rather, having strategic foresight, we can consider possible, probable, and preferred futures (Inayatullah, 2013).

But strategy doesn't live in a PowerPoint. It lives in how well the next layer of leaders, employees, and stakeholders understand it, believe in it, and act on it. (See Chapter 13 – Stakeholder Alignment)

You can have the best plan in the world, but if the people around you don't see the play or know where their piece fits, it falls over. The smartest leadership teams don't just plan the move—they choreograph the whole board. That's how you embed strategy. You operationalise it by helping everyone play their role in the bigger game.

Gain buy-in from senior leaders and incorporate their feedback; diverse perspectives and input into the strategy is crucial. It is important that key senior stakeholders are engaged and can influence and shape strategy. Bring senior leaders together to connect to the strategy. Create an environment where open, respectful dialogue can surface diverse views, link strategy to the work happening every day, and shape the future you're heading towards. Most importantly, use this time to strengthen connections among senior leaders.

Once we have created a strategy, we need to create some structure to confirm the goals we are focusing on and how we will measure success.

Goal setting

Once you are clear on the strategy, you can determine how to operationalise the strategy by setting goals to get there. You will have long- and short-term goals that align with the strategy. When everything is important, nothing is, so you need to be strategic on what the fundamental priorities are. Otherwise, people will be overloaded and nothing will get done.

Leaders need to guide the team and individuals to focus on the right things. It is important to be clear about what success looks like if you achieve those goals. This could be as simple as having SMART goals—i.e. goals that are specific, measurable, achievable, relevant, and time-bound.

OKRs

A great goal-setting framework to bring the strategy to life is OKRs. OKRs are qualitative 'Objectives' that have quantitative measures of success known as a 'Key Result' to achieve the strategy. I cover OKRs in detail in *Thriving Leaders*.

Objectives: What do we want to achieve?
Key results: How are we going to measure our success?
Initiatives: What are we going to do to achieve it?

It is about gaining focus on the two to three most important objectives and doing these well, measured by two to five key results for each objective. Create measurable key results for each objective. Ensure they are both outcome-based and time-bound.

Leaders run the risk of trying to do everything. More and more, I'm hearing senior teams feeling they have been given impossible goals or tasks by executives or boards. People feel overwhelmed, burnt out, and disengaged as a result. At times, leaders need to learn how to push back, influence priorities, explain the trade-offs and risks of pushing that hard. This can feel very risky, like your job is on the line. Velasquez and Starrk in their *Harvard Business Review* article, 'When You're Asked to Meet Impossible Goals', share the Strategic Refusal Matrix. This 2x2 matrix looks at execution feasibility and strategic importance:

- If feasibility and strategic importance are both low, decline and justify why—reframe it as reprioritisation.

- If feasibility is low but strategic importance is high, renegotiate the timeline or resources, highlighting the trade-offs.
- If feasibility is high but strategic importance is low, deprioritise it and redirect focus to initiatives of higher importance.
- If both are high, commit and focus resources to execute.

This can help narrow your focus, so your energy is spent on what is truly important and team members are not spread too thin.

Communicating strategy and goals

Leaders need to learn how to communicate strategy with conviction so that their teams understand it, and know how they can contribute. Teams should be involved in defining the pathway required to achieve the strategic vision in their area; those that do will have more buy-in.

Storytelling is key to making strategy stick. It turns abstract plans into something people remember and connect to. As a leader, you need to be able to articulate how your team contributes to the overall strategy. If you're in the most senior team in the organisation or business unit, your job is to bring it to life for your people. Develop a strategy narrative that explains the 'from—to' shift, integrates the why, and how, and explains what is unique about your strategy. It needs to be succinct, memorable, and repeatable by leaders within the organisation.

If you're leading a team, help them see how their day-to-day work fits into the bigger picture and how they're making a difference. Check that what your team is focused on aligns with the strategy. When people can see the link between their work and the bigger goal, it makes the work more meaningful and helps the strategy come to life.

Monitoring and reviewing

Establish a regular cadence for checking in on progress towards your OKRs, or your team goals (quarterly or monthly). Assign ownership; have someone accountable for tracking and report progress.

Claire DeCarteret from Gallup recommended on the *Thriving Leaders Podcast*: "Thriving teams measure what they treasure. Measure the right things. Not everything that can be counted counts. It's what Einstein said. What you measure gets managed." I agree, you need to be clear on what your most important metrics are to measure to know that you have been successful with the goals you are trying to achieve.

Your team needs a clear operating rhythm to stay on track with strategic goals. For senior teams, consider a strategy dashboard. Build regular reporting into your rhythm. Strategy isn't set and forget. You want to check in on progress at least quarterly.

Just don't mix up BAU KPIs and OKRs—they serve different purposes. KPIs track operational health. OKRs track strategic progress. You need both, but don't merge them.

When you meet, don't just read through the numbers. The purpose is to tell the story that the data is revealing. What did we achieve? Where did we struggle? What does this mean? Where do we go from here? Get the team talking. Let the data inform a discussion that drives decisions and shapes the next quarter.

There is the saying that culture eats strategy for breakfast. Leaders can keep teams focused on results by building in simple mechanisms: clear goals, visible outcomes, transparent reporting, and recognition that reinforces results. Strategy isn't just a plan, it's a practice. How you communicate, behave, and build it into the day-to-day operating rhythm influences the team's ability to achieve the strategy.

CHAPTER 7

Team Accountability

*Teams that commit to decisions and standards
of performance do not hesitate to hold one
another accountable.*

— Patrick Lencioni

Once you have a strategy and goals in place, it's time to focus on the team's accountability.

I like to consider accountability like a river. Like a river, accountability begins at its source—a task, a person, a project, or a strategy to be achieved. The river's flow is the steady action needed to meet that goal. When expectations are clear and responsibility is taken, the water runs smoothly. But, like rocks or fallen trees in a river, challenges arise and must be navigated. Streams join the main flow, just as stakeholders or managers contribute to a project—adding strength or increasing pressure.

A river sustains an entire ecosystem; accountability does the same. When the water is polluted, everyone downstream feels the impact. And just as a river meets the sea at its delta, true accountability ends with delivery—the outcome achieved and the promise kept.

A culture of accountability

A culture of accountability is created, one ripple at a time. Like a ripple in water, it begins with the individual, a small splash which then builds momentum through shared team effort and ultimately influences the collective system, the whole organisation.

To create a culture of accountability, you need the following three elements:

1. **Individual accountability:** The psychological ownership of your individual performance and behaviours to deliver on an outcome.
2. **Shared accountability:** Shared goals and outcomes between people within teams.
3. **Collective accountability:** Systemic between teams and stakeholders within an organisation.

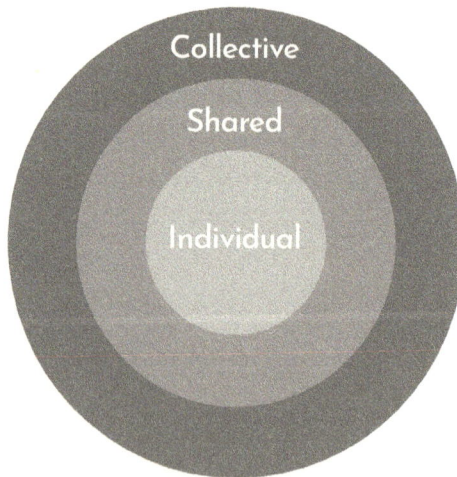

This may feel idealistic; however, it is required for a culture of accountability. Extensive studies have looked at these three constructs of accountability separately. I believe it is the combination of these that creates a culture of accountability. How they interrelate influences how teams and organisations perform, the level of psychological safety, the learning culture, and outcomes.

When an organisation has a culture of accountability, individuals and teams understand what is expected of each other. There is strong psychological safety, and this leads to improved performance, trust, transparency, and problem-solving. Creating an accountability culture is an ongoing process that requires commitment and effort.

A workplace accountability study by Culture Partners, surveying over 40,000 people across industries, found that most organisations are failing to establish clear accountability at an individual, team, and organisational level. Among employees, 82% avoid or fail to hold others accountable.

🌐 REAL-WORLD CASE STUDY

Be clear to be kind

Insync treat accountability as a relationship skill. Leaders set clear expectations, use scorecards, and give timely feedback— so people know what good looks like and where to adjust. Be specific, be regular, and be human.

As Jeremy Summers shared on the *Thriving Leaders Podcast*:

"Accountability at Insync is something we take seriously, but we approach it with care. For us, the crossover between accountability and relationships is really key. We don't get confused between being kind and being nice. For us, being kind means giving regular, clear feedback and holding each other to the expectations we've agreed on. That helps us avoid blind spots and keeps our culture strong.

Everyone has a scorecard, so it's clear what success looks like. We hold people accountable for the things they can control—if someone's doing the work and the outcomes just aren't there because of external factors, we support them. Micromanaging is the enemy of accountability.

We trust our people to do the work in the way that works best for them. We don't need to see them doing it—we measure outcomes, not hours. That trust shows up in the way we lead and in the way we coach. We promise our people regular one-on-ones, real development conversations, and support to grow. But they're expected to show up too. Accountability at Insync isn't top-down—it's mutual."

Clarity is fundamental to accountability. Performance standards are clear and teams are trusted to deliver.

To create a culture of accountability, it requires this ripple effect between individual, shared, and collective accountability. Moving from 'I', to 'we', to 'us'.

Individual accountability

Individual accountability is at the centre of the ripple; without it, nothing happens. When we are individually accountable, we take ownership and personal responsibility. The word 'take' is important; we don't feel like it has been forced upon us, we are choosing to take it on. This subtle difference empowers individuals and helps to shift it into a privilege and power.

On the *Thriving Leaders Podcast*, David Clutterbuck suggests we should rebrand accountability as "ownership". On another *Thriving Leaders Podcast* episode, Amy Edmondson defined it as the amount of "psychological ownership" that one has. To build on this, it is the psychological ownership of your performance and behaviours to deliver an outcome. When we are accountable, we feel empowered to take action and follow through. We understand what is expected of us, or if we don't, we clarify expectations. We learn from our mistakes and are open to taking on feedback to improve and achieve the outcome. Individually, we need agency. Agency to be autonomous, set goals for ourselves, and articulate where we will focus.

Leaders must role model individual accountability. Your team will notice when you don't follow through on your commitments. Acknowledge when you make mistakes or haven't upheld the commitments you have set. Be clear about when and how you will achieve what was agreed.

There may seem to be a reluctance for people to be accountable. They are already busy, so they may not want the additional pressure to take on more. They also may fear making a mistake and want to focus on things they know they can achieve to save face. We want to be viewed as competent and doing a good job, so at times people may hide when they haven't followed through on expectations.

If you are individually accountable, you are clear on what you have committed to, so you can focus on your goals.

Holding individuals accountable

As a leader you are required to hold others accountable. In Gallup's 2025 *State of the Global Workplace Report,* only 45% of employees report they clearly know what is expected of them. In the *Harvard Business Review* article, 'How to actually encourage employee accountability' (2020), they found that 82% of managers acknowledge they have limited to no ability to hold others accountable successfully, and 91% of employees would say that "effectively holding others accountable" is one of their company's top leadership-development needs.

You don't want to be perceived as micromanaging your people. Leaders want to be liked and maintain strong relationships with their team members. As the leader, be aware of how you are contributing to a perceived lack of accountability. Let's discuss how you can hold individuals accountable.

The 4Cs of accountability

In my first book, *Thriving Leaders*, there is a whole chapter dedicated to accountability. We unpack the barriers to accountability and what to do when there is a perceived lack of accountability. I introduce a 4Cs model to help hold others accountable. The 4Cs stand for Capability, Clear Expectations, Checking in, and Communicating Outcomes.

Capability: Assessing team members' capability when delegating work or upskilling, if someone doesn't have the skills.

Clear expectations: Articulating the outcome and the measure of success is key to providing clarity. This will include why they are doing something, how and what's expected of them, and by when. Asking your team member to play back what they are going to do in their own words gives you the assurance that they have understood and that you are on the same page.

Checking in: Create mechanisms to check in with your people, to provide support, feedback, and a clear cadence. Communicating how you will check in with a team member balances autonomy without micromanagement. Agreeing to this upfront is useful.

Communicating outcomes: We should embrace consequences; however, this is a C-word people seem to hate. Consequences can be both positive and negative. Accountability requires consequences, so people have skin in the game. Communicating outcomes includes reinforce (when things go well), redo (when things need to improve), and release (when someone hasn't met expectations).

To have a thriving team, individuals need to feel a sense of ownership for their individual responsibilities and for the shared outcomes of the team. Be open and share your expectations with your team. Ambiguity can lead to underperformance and slow decision-making. When expectations aren't clear, it is more difficult to hold people accountable.

Shared accountability

From the first splash of individual accountability, the ripple moves outwards between people. Shared accountability is how we hold each other accountable within a team for achieving shared goals, performance standards, and outcomes. It requires trust between individuals and psychological safety within the team to raise concerns when someone hasn't followed through on their commitments for the greater good of the team. This is very hard to do if there aren't strong relationships, or when we are not clear on the shared goals, if there is an unclear direction, or the team's work is not visible.

When there is a lack of accountability within a team, it can cause people to pursue their own agendas, look after their own 'patch', and let egos come into play, or engage in office politics. People hold back, go quiet, and start focusing on themselves for self-preservation. There are no consequences when people don't follow through on their commitments. It becomes either a taboo subject, or people become nice and don't acknowledge the repeated behaviour of a team member not picking up their slack. Even worse, things build up and then, when someone does try to address the lack of follow-through, they explode. The pace and sequence of the work are important. You may also realise that people may be avoiding the work and not taking accountability for their part.

> *This is a story about four people named Everybody, Somebody, Anybody, and Nobody. There was an important job to be done, and Everybody was sure that Somebody would do it. Anybody could have done it, but Nobody did it. Somebody got angry about that, because it was Everybody's job. Everybody thought Anybody could do it, but Nobody realised that Everybody wouldn't do it. It ended up that Everybody blamed Somebody when Nobody did what Anybody could have.*
>
> — Anonymous

This is an excellent story of where there was a lack of accountability, and unclear roles and responsibilities so nothing was accomplished. Sounds familiar within a team. When team members feel that there is a lack of accountability, others need to pick up the slack.

In a team, a lack of accountability can happen when there is no clear vision or strategy of where you are heading or committing to too much rather than defining what is most important. Unclear or overlapping roles and responsibilities or being completely limited with resources can impact accountability. The team must have clear expectations of what is expected from a performance and a behaviour perspective. Clear expectations allow teams to hold one another accountable and ensure the team has a common goal.

In Project Aristotle, Google discovered that 'dependability' was the second most important factor in determining team effectiveness. This is why having psychological safety and accountability within a team are two of the most important factors contributing to a team's effectiveness. They are intrinsically linked. If team members don't feel safe, they won't take ownership. They will put their head down and deliver in their patch, self-protect by staying in their own lane. This often feels like the team is operating in silos and not in a unified way. When people are afraid of failing or making mistakes, they tend to deflect, avoid, or hide. It takes vulnerability to put your hand up and say, "I stuffed up." But most people want to be seen as competent and capable. So, when things go pear-shaped, they hide it.

Team members must hold each other accountable. It requires peer accountability where team members monitor each other's performance, and are open to feedback. This does not get the leader off the hook, however; it is the responsibility of every member to hold each other accountable. The leader still needs to hold ultimate accountability within the team.

Distribution of authority and mutual accountability across the team means it is shared among peers. There is a willingness to collaborate and problem-solve together, through ongoing relationships and dialogue.

⊕ REAL-WORLD CASE STUDY

Raising the bar with respect at AFCA

At AFCA, Greg Pickering inherited highly engaged teams with some serious performance challenges. When he took over, one team had 100% engagement, the other 80% engagement— but they weren't meeting expectations. Some people were producing very little work, and it wasn't just about volume. The work they were doing didn't align with the organisation's values. It was technical and legalistic, which made it inaccessible to a wider audience. And that matters when you're working with real people in crisis.

As Greg shared on the *Thriving Leaders Podcast*:

"We went slow. I started by listening and asking questions. People shared that career progression felt out of reach and work wasn't being allocated fairly. So we addressed both. We created bespoke career pathways—and we used data to dig into work allocation. What we found was confronting."

There was a feeling in the team that some people were getting easier work—and when he looked at the data, they were right. The simpler files were being funnelled to a few individuals, and it was masking underperformance.

"I pulled the data apart—case by case—to understand what was really going on. That gave us the evidence we needed to change the allocation model. And when people questioned the shift, I could explain it clearly. They didn't have to like it. But they understood the 'why'—and that's what helped them get on board."

Once expectations were reset, they had to operationalise them. That meant clarity around targets, shared definitions of quality, and a consistent approach to feedback. They introduced clear expectations—what good looks like—and held everyone to the same standard. That meant having performance conversations, including with the leader, who ultimately chose to step away. Some others self-selected out too. But those who stayed felt the shift immediately.

"They felt seen. They felt heard. They felt it was finally fair. It wasn't about micro-managing—it was about fairness. Everyone knew what 'good' looked like. And everyone was measured against the same standards. That gave us a foundation to build trust, to recognise performance, and to keep lifting as a team.

Performance lifted. We went from 70–90% of expectations to 150% and above—and it's sustained. Because the people who are here want to be here, they know what's expected of them. And they know I've got their back."

This is a great example of using data and conversations to understand what's really going on. To gain clarity and commitment through their core value of fairness.

Holding each other accountable

It is human nature to overestimate our level of accountability compared to the people around us. Decades of research show that most people rate their own performance, commitment, and reliability far higher than their peers or managers do. The science tells us that this is based on our self-serving bias, as we attribute individual success to internal factors, such as our skills and effort, and attribute failures to external factors, like bad luck. This demonstrates that we believe we are doing our bit, while we finger-point and blame others. We judge ourselves on our intentions and challenges, and judge others on their behaviour, often holding an imperfect view of others' actions. This common disconnect means that we see ourselves carrying the weight of accountability, and those around us not pulling their weight. In thriving teams, we need to recognise this tendency.

Thriving teams are transparent about individual and shared accountabilities. Goals are visible, and it is clear about the interdependencies between team members' work. Performance standards are clear, and team members are involved in decision-making processes, so they have more buy-in and clarity on the desired outcomes.

We need to make our work more transparent and visible so that people can hold each other accountable, rather than hiding what they're working on. When people know what others are working on, accountability gets easier. Positive peer pressure is effective.

However, it only works when there is trust and safety, allowing individuals to challenge and support one another. When we create the right conditions, our teams will stretch, grow, and own their work. I believe that a little bit of peer pressure can actually be beneficial. When people know their work is visible, and they trust the people around them, they're more likely to follow through. They don't want to let the team down. If your team doesn't feel like they've got each other's backs, they'll play it safe. And we all know that no one builds a thriving team in isolation.

When I set out to run 10 kms for the first time, I had an accountability buddy—my friend Catherine. I also shared my progress on Strava with my brother and sister, both seasoned runners. They gave me feedback, based on the data, that helped me tweak my approach. I hit my 13-week goal in just three weeks—albeit I was running very slowly. So, I refined the goal: run 10 kms in under an hour. I got there, thanks to the help and support of my brother James and his groodle, Mav.

When we have feedback loops, we learn, as long as we stay open to new ideas and ways of doing things. When our goals are visible and transparent, we create an environment that supports growth. Tracking progress through data matters—it's motivating and grounding.

Peer pressure works. It can be a powerful motivator—you don't want to let others down. If I hadn't broadcast my commitment to run 10 km in under an hour, I probably would have moved on to something else. Autonomy gives people the responsibility to hold themselves accountable.

Lessons I've learnt:

- Some challenges feel bigger at the start than they actually are.

- When we hit our goals, we need to pause and celebrate the win.
- Progress is often found in refining and building on the goal that came before.

Peer accountability provides:

- Transparency and visibility of work.
- Self-report on progress to peers keeps you on track.
- Healthy peer pressure incentivises people to work hard on deliverables.
- Autonomy gives people the responsibility to hold themselves accountable.

Establish mechanisms in meetings to regularly check in on progress against our shared accountability as a team. This will build a rhythm to highlight successes and share challenges and roadblocks so the team works through them together. If we want better performance, we need better conversations. In thriving teams, people own their mistakes when they haven't followed through on a commitment, and work together to determine how the outcome can be achieved.

Normalise feedback within the team so that it is expected and comes from a good place with positive intentions, such as wanting their peers to learn and grow. Discuss as a team how each person likes to receive feedback, so each team member is aware of preferences. This also signals that feedback is part of how we operate as a team. Peer accountability requires strong relationships in place, anchored in trust and psychological safety, so when a peer calls someone out, it isn't personal, it's not about singling them out, it's about working together to lift the performance standard. This is when people have each other's backs and are calling things out for the greater good of the team. A fear of negative consequences is what stops this from happening within a team.

As the leader of the team, acknowledge examples of consistent accountability by team members to positively reinforce this behaviour. If there is an individual who consistently isn't accountable, refer to the individual accountability section. In my book *Thriving Leaders*, I share some practical tools to do this effectively if this feels like a skill gap for you.

Create accountability buddies within teams for key goals. In my leadership development programs I always get people who don't work together to become accountability buddies. This means that they catch up in between our sessions to check in on their goals, build relationships, and work through challenges together.

The American Society of Training and Development found that when we share our goals with someone else we have a 65% chance of achieving them. This likelihood increases to 95% when we regularly meet with that person about our goals. This is why having one-on-ones and team meetings is so important for your team. Accountability buddies can still apply within teams, where team members have accountability meetings to achieve goals together. Ensure that they are targeted to the goals that each individual team members is trying to achieve. I find this works best in pairs or threes.

Collective accountability

Collective accountability is when each person in an organisation has a One Team mindset. They make decisions for the greater good of the organisation rather than for themselves as an individual or a team. It's no longer about putting your head down and delivering only individually or as a team. It becomes about the shared outcomes for the organisation. Collective accountability is system-wide ownership across teams, functions, and stakeholders.

In organisations where there isn't collective accountability, teams work in isolation, like islands doing their own thing, further driving silos. There is finger-pointing and blame cultures, and this flows then into individuals and teams not taking accountability, as the focus is on 'us' and 'them'. Collective accountability drives engagement, team alignment, and builds relationships through collaboration, trust, and transparency. Research from the *International Journal of Conflict Management* found that collective accountability drives diverse perspectives, reduces groupthink, and promotes shared responsibility.

Collective accountability requires unity. A shared identity and intention which is anchored in core values and the culture within the organisation. It requires knowledge sharing, collaboration, and sharing problems. The challenge is often competing priorities, role clarity, and communication breakdowns.

After facilitating a Senior Leader Forum for a client on 'The Art of Accountability', the Chief People Officer shared after the session, "Our Everybody, Somebody, Anybody, and Nobody story now has a different spin on it! Everyone knows what needs to be done. Someone always takes the initiative. Anyone feels empowered to contribute. And nobody is left wondering who's responsible!"

We can learn a lot from Australia's First Nations culture, which look at the individual in the context of we and us. When they look to the collective, it is about the community, land, ancestors, and future generations—it's big-picture thinking. It is far more holistic, relational, and restorative than Western culture—all things which would shape a more harmonious and inclusive culture within organisations.

We will pick this up in detail in Chapter 13 – Stakeholder Alignment, where we will deep dive into stakeholder alignment.

The ripple of accountability starts at the source—an individual's accountability. This requires us to look in the mirror at the psychological ownership, commitments, and responsibility we take on to follow through. Shared accountability happens between peers within a team. It requires shared goals, psychological safety, and transparency at work. This way we can hold each other accountable. Collective accountability is systemic and cultural. It's the way we align, collaborate, and deliver together. The ripple of accountability starts with 'I', grows through the team to 'we', and flows through the system to 'us'.

Accountability

A thriving team needs a clear direction. A north star they are working towards. This could be a strategy if you are the most senior team in the organisation or goals that help contribute towards the strategy. It's important once this strategy or goals are created that you create an operating rhythm to track progress against the things that are most important to achieve.

The river of accountability flows through every individual, every team, and every layer in the organisation. When it is clear, we work together to remove barriers and we can achieve more than we expect. Having clarity about what each individual in your team is accountable for, shared accountability between team members, and collective accountability between other teams and key stakeholders increases this level of achievement. How will you create this ripple within your team?

What thriving teams do differently:

- Have a clear direction with input from the team.
- Understand their individual, shared, and collective accountability.
- Hold each other accountable to commitments, goals, and behaviours.

Actions

1. **Co-create a strategy or shared goals for the team.** If you are the most senior team in the organisation, or business unit, create a strategy. If you are not, then co-create team goals that align with the organisational or business unit strategy.

2. **Connect daily work to the strategy.** Ensure team members understand how their work contributes towards the strategy. Make the connection.

3. **Monitor and review progress against team goals.** Create an operating rhythm and make the work and measures of success visible.

4. **Start the ripple.** Set the context that individual and shared accountability are required for the team to be successful. Explain that accountability is a privilege. Be accountable. Demonstrate the importance.

5. **Hold each other accountable.** Teach the team the skills to hold one another accountable. Hold others accountable using the 4Cs.

RESOURCES

www.thrivingculture.com.au/ttbook

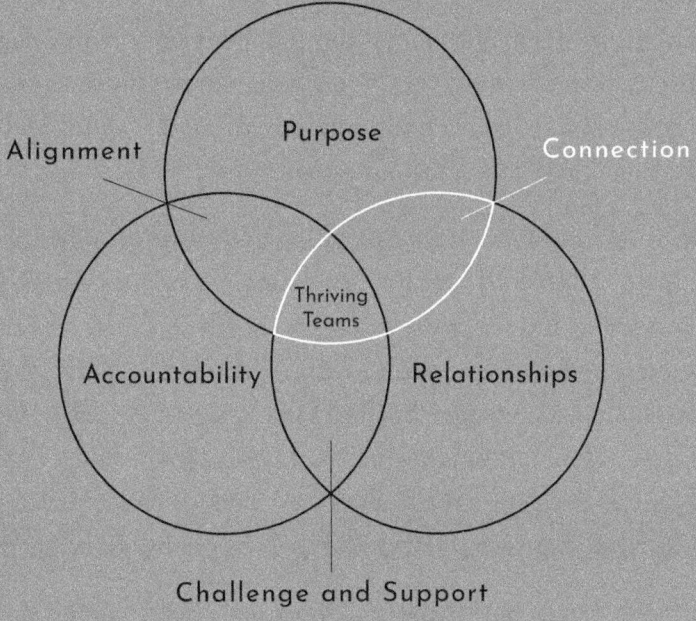

Alignment

Purpose

Connection

Thriving
Teams

Accountability

Relationships

Challenge and Support

Connection sits between Purpose and Relationships in the Thriving Teams Model. This is because thriving teams have meaningful and purposeful connections, simple team processes and ways of working, and a sense of togetherness, even when teams are dispersed either geographically or through remote working.

Thriving teams create opportunities for the team to come together and discuss what is important. They collaborate with purpose. It is how teams connect, solve problems, and make decisions, and share information, knowledge, resources, and ideas.

Connection is how we create meaning and purpose. We are tribal creatures and want to feel like we belong. Creating some simple team processes and ways of working provides certainty and rhythm that team members can expect. This helps team members collaborate and build relationships beyond their day-to-day work. We need to be even more intentional in creating cohesive and connected teams as we navigate hybrid work and greater stresses outside of work. Thriving teams have meaningful and purposeful connections.

Connection drives performance and productivity. A study of 1,106 US office workers on high-performing teams found that connection was a key factor in what high-performing teams do differently (*Harvard Business Review*, 2021). These are the five key things that high-performing teams do differently:

- They are not afraid to pick up the phone.
- They are more strategic with their meetings.
- They invest time bonding over non-work topics.
- They give and receive appreciation more frequently.
- They are more authentic at work.

These are not expensive things to invest in and really don't take much more time given the return they yield.

Connection within a team needs to be an ongoing focus. Thriving teams create continuous momentum to build strong bonds with each other. This means being intentional with building team connection. It's how teams stay aligned and in sync, especially in hybrid or dispersed teams. We cover the benefits and importance of this in depth in Part 2 – Relationships.

Teams are complex social systems. We are not just managing tasks, but people's energy, emotions, habits, and quirks. Connection holds the system together.

Connection in a team is like music; you need both the beat and the notes.

Togetherness is the beat, the emotional pulse. Shared stories, laughter, checking in with each other when it's been a tough week. This human rhythm gives the team energy and tempo. You feel it, it's how you stay in sync emotionally. It creates the team's culture.

The notes are the team processes and ways of working. It's the working rhythm, the operating rhythm, how you meet, communicate, make decisions to get the work done.

The beat without notes—you have a great vibe, but no song. The notes without a beat, well, that is just noise. Real connection is the groove that happens only when the beat and notes come together. That's when a team makes music.

This part of the book focuses on togetherness and team processes.

CHAPTER 8

Togetherness

Coming together is a beginning;
keeping together is progress;
working together is success.

— Henry Ford

Togetherness is the quality time you spend together as a team. To deepen our connection and improve our ability to collaborate, we need to build a sense of togetherness by getting to know each other beyond the work, on a deeper human level. Relationships are built when we spend time together, but we don't always have the luxury of being face to face. High-performing teams communicate regularly, even if they are not physically together.

It can be more challenging to build trust with a team that has been newly formed or is working apart from one another. Be more conscious of creating these opportunities to build trust. Teams are always evolving; people come and go; teams are not static. Ensure that when you bring new team members into the team, share the journey that you have been on—challenges and successes.

Trust within hybrid teams requires a level of autonomy. When employees have autonomy to decide how the work should be done, it creates engagement and retention. This means leaders need to manage for outcomes and not hours. When operating in a hybrid team, we need to be intentional to create moments of connection.

There are several exercises you can perform to help build trust, get to know each other beyond the work, and fast-track the time you spend together.

⚙️ TEAM IN PRACTICE

The revolving door

A fast-growing tech scale-up had ambitious plans to dominate its market. But inside the leadership team, stability was rare. Senior leaders came and went as investors pushed for results and the pressure to scale mounted. Just as the team found its rhythm, another leader would resign or be replaced, forcing everyone to reset.

The constant churn created exhaustion and instability. Priorities shifted with each new leader, strategies were half implemented, and staff became sceptical of change. The cycle of building momentum only to start over again left the leadership team disheartened.

The CEO described it this way:

- "It feels like we're building a house of cards—every time we get close, someone pulls one out."
- "We're stuck in survival mode instead of scaling mode."
- "The pace is relentless, and turnover just adds to the chaos."

The shift came when the leadership team decided to create stability through connection and trust. They invested in getting to know each other beyond the work—through leadership offsites, structured conversations about values and purpose, and intentionally building one-to-one relationships. This helped them build a shared identity and commit to operating as one team. They shifted their focus onto shared priorities, a strong operating rhythm, and consistent systems, holding steady on these. This reduced the impact of high turnover, strengthened retention, and gave the team the resilience to stay united despite the turbulence around them.

Ways to get to know each other beyond the work

Find opportunities for team members to share more about themselves.

Quick rituals

Start your team meeting on a topic unrelated to work. This is useful as everyone has spoken and has a voice so they are more likely to contribute in the meeting. Plus you get to know people on a deeper level. All you need is five minutes. Topics could include:

- Best holiday or worst holiday ever.
- Hobbies or interests.
- Favourite or worst foods.
- Favourite movie and why.
- What TV show you are bingeing.
- Favourite book and why.
- Favourite childhood memory.
- What you wanted to be when you grew up.
- If I was to open the boot of your car what is the weirdest thing I would find?

Deeper activities

When you have more time, a quarterly or trimester rhythm, try some group activities to get to know each other on a deeper personal level. A team offsite is an ideal setting to do this. If your budget allows, choose a space outside of the office; this minimises distractions and stops people's minds wandering into the day-to-day or the temptation to do work in breaks.

Activities could include:

- Each team member shares a personal story and how it has shaped them into the person they are today.
- Each team member shares a career-defining moment.
- Create a life-on-a-page where team members collate photos on a page and share what the pictures mean to them.
- Get each team member to bring in an object that is meaningful to them. Let them share why.
- Share a nostalgic childhood memory that has had an impact on you.

For other conversation prompts, check out our Thriving Teams Connection Cards on www.thrivingculture.com.au

Understand personality styles

Appreciating different personality styles so that teams understand and value their similarities and differences creates an inclusive team. When I work with teams, I start with a personality profiling tool. I like to use Facet5, as it looks at your innate personality, and considers how that influences behaviour. This helps to build individual self-awareness, as well as using the team report, which provides valuable insights into each other. The reason this is so powerful is that it creates a platform for a rich discussion about how the team is operating based on their natural preferences, how effectively the team is working together, and how natural behavioural styles help or hinder the team's effectiveness.

THOUGHT LEADER INSIGHTS

Understanding different personalities

Grant Gemmell is the Managing Director of Facet5 Global, a leading personality profiling organisation.

Teams move faster when people can name how they prefer to think and work. A personality profile doesn't lock people into boxes; instead, it provides a lens for understanding behaviour across time, situations, and contexts. It gives us a shared language that makes the invisible visible. With that language, people can describe how they turn up at work, what energises them, and why things happen the way they do.

When you create that intuitive language, you also create a bridge of understanding. It becomes a kind of scaffolding that helps people make sense of themselves and others. With it, teams can build trust more quickly, strengthen relationships, and collaborate with greater ease. Differences don't disappear— but they become easier to talk about and to work with.

On the *Thriving Leaders Podcast*, Grant explained:

"Everybody has a personality. A great personality instrument should deal with the nuance, create curiosity, and help people see the patterns in how they think, decide, and relate. It's not about labels or excuses, but about insight and awareness."

That awareness creates choices. Instead of being trapped by type, people gain the confidence to flex their approach in different contexts. They become more curious about others, and more conscious of their impact. The outcome is better collaboration, faster problem-solving, and communication that feels more open and honest.

Key learnings: Use personality as a lens, not a label. With a shared language we create scaffolding for trust, sense-making, and collaboration. Used well, personality increases curiosity, deepens relationships, and helps people work together more effectively.

Understand individual and team strengths

Another great tool is the Gallup 34 *Strengths Report* and using the Team Grid as a tool to understand when team members are at their best, and how they can leverage their strengths together. Discuss the different strengths across the team and how you can play to each other's strengths. Claire DeCarteret in the *Thriving Leaders Podcast* suggests that with strengths we need to "name it, claim it, and aim it". Know your strengths, build efficacy around them, then point them at performance or purpose so you have an impact.

If you don't have access to tools like this, go back and look at your results from the Values in Action survey (VIA). (See Chapter 2 – Team Purpose) Collate the top five strengths of the team. Look at signature strengths that sit across the team and discuss how you can leverage these.

Get to know your team on a personal level—what drives them, what motivates them, and what frustrates them. Have discussions with your team about these things—individually and collectively. The team will see similarities and differences, and start to value them.

Neurodiversity

Neurodiversity refers to the natural variation in human cognition. These conditions include autism spectrum disorder (ASD), ADHD, and dyslexia. Globally, 15–25% of the workforce is estimated to be neurodivergent; however, it is likely higher, as some people choose not to disclose this information to employers.

Recent research suggests that teams with neurodivergent people can be 30% more productive and 30% more innovative when roles align with unique strengths. However, psychological safety needs to be present. Often neurodivergent people need workplace accommodations to be successful and play to their strengths. This may mean disclosing this information to managers and team members. Be mindful of neurodiversity within your team. Leverage the strengths of all team members.

Shared experiences

Relationships are built through shared experiences. Creating opportunities for these experiences is important, whether that's social connection, team challenges, or collaborative activities.

Research from Cornell University found the benefits of breaking bread together. There is a link to better performance in teams that eat together, which is rooted in anthropology—a social glue that binds us. Shared meals, where we pass plates, give us a sense of family and help build trust and connection. Enjoy a meal together—whether that's breakfast, lunch, or dinner.

Do something fun as a team: outdoor walks, yoga, meditation, a puzzle escape room, painting class, team volunteering, a beach clean, or an amazing race scavenger hunt through the city. Just think of something that will include everyone. It's the balance of pushing people outside their comfort zone without excluding people's physical abilities.

The reality is that some activities will resonate more than others based on preferences, so mix up the themes of these activities. Another leader shared that they rotate who picks the activities in their team, as it's hard to please everyone. This way, you get a diverse range of fun activities, since not everyone will enjoy them all.

Another great shared experience is attending a relevant conference, event, or ESG activity together. Learning together is a great shared experience.

Team reflections

Create opportunities for team reflection regularly. These activities build bonds as individuals show vulnerability and disclose information. Here are some ideas to adopt:

- **Proudest moment:** Invite each person to share the one thing they're most proud of with the team. It's a positive, uplifting activity that gets people thinking about what's gone well.
- **Our story exercise:** This is a simple but powerful way to shape the team narrative. It's particularly useful if you've got a mix of long-standing team members and newer arrivals. It helps bring closure to the past and allows you to be intentional about the story you want to create going forward.
- **Team feedback:** One exercise I run is to have team members give each other feedback. There is often a sense of apprehension when asked to provide feedback on your peers; however, when facilitated well, this is a powerful exercise which has real impact on the team's effectiveness. I suggest first making sure everyone's confident with the basics of delivering feedback. If you need to develop your feedback capability, check out my first book, *Thriving Leaders.* You can do this feedback session as a group, or get more personal with a 'speed dating' style set-up: pair team members for 10 minutes to share what each person brings to the team that they value, and one thing they could either improve or stop doing for the benefit of the team. Do this a couple of times a year to create a culture of feedback.

When you are not physically together

Togetherness is also about the quality of the time you spend when you are not physically together. This includes virtual interactions, phone calls, texts, emails, and instant messages. Thriving teams communicate regularly, even if they are not physically together.

🌐 REAL-WORLD CASE STUDY

Remote work means we connect intentionally

Insync have created intentional activities for their team that is remote to ensure connection and a sense of togetherness.

On the *Thriving Leaders Podcast*, Jeremy Summers shared some of the activities Insync uses to build connection.

"Remote work's not something we're casual about—it takes effort. The less we see of each other, the more deliberate we have to be about connection. So, we treat connection as real work. We run coffee roulettes where people are randomly paired up to have a chat—about anything. We've got business monthlies that everyone attends, and we run a session called A Chance to Grow, where people present to the rest of the business. It gives people a voice, and it helps us all learn. We've even got an event called Insync Connected, where we invite people's families to join us for an afternoon to say thanks. That togetherness—that's our secret sauce."

How can you create intentional and purposeful ways to connect as a team?

Thriving teams speak positively on behalf of each other when a team member isn't present, whether it is about the work area or the person themselves. This could be how a team member represents the whole team when they are with a stakeholder. Or how a team member represents a different part of the team. This is where the team needs to be a unified front, speak with conviction, and support their team members. Thriving teams operate in a unified way even when they are not physically together.

CHAPTER 9

Team Processes

Efficiency means doing things correctly while effectiveness means selecting the right tasks and combined they establish effective teamwork.

— Peter Drucker

Thriving teams connect with purpose through simple team processes and ways of working. Developing these processes helps people know what to expect—whether that's meeting rhythms, workflows, or how the team gets things done.

Operating rhythms

An operating rhythm creates a repeatable cadence, so team members know what to expect each day, week, month, and year. It creates certainty and removes ambiguity. It's important that the operating rhythm is adhered to and prioritised. If we are always chopping and changing, then team members don't feel like the team is valued. This demonstrates the importance you place on the team. It provides certainty, structure, and clear expectations.

Every team's operating rhythm will be different to suit their context and culture. Teams need to develop a cohesive operating rhythm that allows for collaboration, information sharing, problem-solving, and decision-making. This ensures that team members are on the same page and can get the work done.

Develop a regular meeting schedule that team members can rely on. Consistency in meeting times and structure helps establish a predictable routine, allowing team members to plan their workloads accordingly. This rhythm provides clarity and stability, enabling teams to work together more effectively.

Teams need rituals that reinforce the rhythm and standards of work. This could include stand-up meetings, weekly reflections about wins and learnings, and sharing team successes.

Review your operating rhythm every three to six months to ensure it is still effective. This continuous feedback loop demonstrates that you learn as a team and that you want it to work for everyone.

Meetings

Meetings are an integral part of work. They're a symbol of team and organisational culture. Ineffective meetings are a common challenge, characterised by unproductive, repetitive, and demotivating sessions. Signs of meeting mediocrity include lack of engagement, passive participation, unclear objectives, and no follow-up on actions.

The number of meetings has tripled since 2020. The more senior you are, the more time you spend in them. According to *Cendyn's State of Meetings Report* (2025), executives spend 19–23 hours per week in meetings, managers 16 hours, and individual contributors eight hours. That's a lot of time—so let's make it count.

I'm noticing more people not giving their full attention in meetings. Approximately 73% of people work on other things in meetings, according to the *Microsoft Work Trend Index* (2022). This is exacerbated with working virtually. We all know the feeling: we're in a team meeting, and someone is clearly typing an email or getting pings on Teams. Even worse is when you receive an email from someone while you are in the same meeting! It happens. This even occurs when face to face. People check phones, read emails and text. This 'multitasking' is ineffective, only serving to distract.

Hybrid work has exacerbated people's view that this behaviour is acceptable. It has been normalised, but it's not productive. Nine in 10 people daydream in meetings, according to *Atlassian's State of Teams: Collaboration and Productivity Report* (2025). Their minds wander to their to-do list, which is probably when they end up sneaking in that cheeky email, so there is one less thing on their to-do list.

Despite the challenges of meetings, they can still be valuable if executed well. They provide a platform for collaboration, information sharing, problem-solving, decision-making, relationship-building, and a way to celebrate success. Meetings bring together diverse perspectives, expertise, and insights, allowing teams to tackle complex challenges collectively. The interactive nature of meetings enables brainstorming, idea sharing, and the exchange of different viewpoints that create innovative solutions. They also help to build relationships and connections among team members.

How can we make meetings more engaging so that people stay focused and present?

Team meetings

Clearly define your team meeting's purpose—and communicate it in advance so attendees understand what's expected and how they can contribute.

Common meeting purposes include:

- **Information sharing:** Updates and situational awareness, so everyone's on the same page.
- **Problem-solving:** Unpack challenges, explore causes, and brainstorm solutions.
- **Decision-making:** Agree on the way forward.
- **Co-creation:** Collaborate, share ideas, and input.
- **Strategy and planning:** take a big-picture view, work on the business and plan ahead.
- **Connection:** Build relationships, celebrate wins, and get to know each other.

Keep meetings focused on the purpose. Be clear on agendas and follow up on actions. Use 'parking lots' when meetings get derailed and discussions veer off topic and off on tangents. A parking lot in a meeting is a visible list (whiteboard, flipchart, or shared document) where you list relevant discussion points that need to be revisited in the future. When we spend time discussing irrelevant content, it wastes time, slows down progress to outcomes, and dilutes the value of the meeting itself. Use parking lots to keep meetings on track.

Preparation is key for meetings, especially strategic quarterly meetings. If there is a pre-read to get everyone on the same page, send it with adequate time. If big decisions need to be made, some people naturally will need more time to digest information. Send through reports, presentations, or recommendations that will add value to the discussion. Make sure all pre-read is relevant to not waste team members' time before the meetings even start.

At least quarterly, as a team, review the effectiveness of a meeting, or if you observe that the purpose and effectiveness are wavering, call it out for a discussion so that you can discuss, learn, and improve future meetings.

Meetings often go on for too long. Consider the appropriate length based on the purpose and core agenda items.

Types of meetings

It is important to have a regular meeting rhythm and clear agendas.

Meeting elements usually include:

- **Inform:** Share content, delegate work, allocate resources.
- **Create:** Problem-solve, brainstorm, plan.
- **Decide:** Diagnose the problem, debate it, make decisions.

Your team's rhythm might include:

- **WIPs/Standups:** Short updates, challenges, next steps.
- **Team meetings:** Broader team check-ins and alignment.
- **Operational meetings:** To review delivery and performance.
- **Topic-dependent meetings:** Ad hoc or project-based.
- **Strategy meetings:** Longer-term or big-picture planning.

Not every team needs every type—design a rhythm that works for your context. Limit the number of attendees to the people who need to be there.

Tips for effective meetings

Here are some ideas to create a valuable meeting that people want to attend.

- **Start and end on time:** Respect people's time. It sets the tone.
- **Personal connection:** Begin with something non-work related. It helps people engage and makes participation easier and encourages participation for the rest of the meeting.
- **Clear meeting purpose:** Set it and share it. It keeps things on track.

- **Use time well:** Avoid wasting time on things that could've been in an email.
- **Encourage collaboration:** Invite quieter team members in with questions. Use tools like digital whiteboards, real-time documents or polls in hybrid settings.
- **Meeting observer:** Rotate someone to give feedback on how the meeting ran.
- **Accountability and action:** Make it count. What's the outcome? Ensure there is a follow-up at the next meeting.
- **Quarterly reviews:** Regularly reflect on what's working and what's not.

Implementing these strategies will make your meetings engaging, purposeful, and ones your people want to attend.

Habits and rituals

Rituals build connection and belonging. These can be symbols, habits, or unspoken cues that shape how your team works and connects. Some executive committees or boards have ineffective rituals. They get caught up in the process and pompous nature of being the senior team, and they don't use their time effectively.

In the *Harvard Business Review* article, 'The Surprising Power of Team Rituals', they studied 929 individuals from 60 countries across a range of rituals. These rituals included icebreakers, team check-ins, retrospectives, and formal onboarding processes. They found the teams with more rituals were more engaged, committed to their team's purpose, had higher psychological safety, interpersonal knowledge, and job satisfaction.

In his book *Team Habits*, Charlie Gilkey discusses the benefits of teams creating habits such as how they communicate, make decisions, plan, and set goals.

At Thriving Culture we have created our own habits and rituals for our Monday and Friday meetings:

- **Personal connection:** Five minutes at the start of meetings to check in on non-work related topics. Gets people talking early so they are more likely to participate in the meeting and builds trust.
- **Intentions for the week:** Monday meetings start with "What's the one most important thing you need to achieve this week?" It keeps us focused on what's most important.
- **Wins and learnings:** On Fridays, we share the biggest win and most important learning of the week. Great for reflection and vulnerability.
- **Team success:** On Fridays, we also share the team's success, which drives shared accountability and allows time to celebrate our successes.
- **Gratitude:** We end Friday meetings sharing what we're grateful for, both work and personal. It's a lovely pause before the weekend.

What are the habits and rituals your team has?

One-on-ones

Meet regularly one-on-one with your team. The frequency will be dependent on the individual and the number of direct reports you have. This is the opportunity to catch up on their work, manage performance, and provide feedback. At least quarterly or biannually, discuss their development, focusing on their career aspirations, capabilities they wish to develop, and work on a plan of how they will get there.

Find an operating rhythm that will work for you and your team. Engage them in the process.

Where teams work

We need to build connections no matter where people work. This continues to be a challenge for leaders and teams, especially with the shift to hybrid work post pandemic. It's become more challenging to manage team culture and build relationships when we're not physically together.

Hybrid work

We are living in a paradox. People want the flexibility, and at the same time, crave human connection. What does this mean for leaders trying to build connected, high-performing teams?

There are differing views on whether we are more productive and connected in hybrid work arrangements. The push from some employers to have people back in the office full time is causing tension.

The *Cisco Global Hybrid Work Study* found hybrid work declined—from 63% in 2022 to 47% in 2025—as office mandates grow. Around 72% of organisations now require in-office attendance, with 46% increasing required office days. But productivity is up: 73% of employees say they're more productive with hybrid work—gaining an average of 7.6 hours in a 40-hour week. It's had positive impacts on innovation, culture, and engagement.

Meanwhile, the *Microsoft Work Trend Index* (2024) reports no drop in productivity post remote shift. Their concern is isolation and siloed networks. Contrast that with *Harvard Business Review's* 'Hybrid Still Isn't Working' research, which found hybrid teams struggled with collaboration, learning, connection, and performance.

Hybrid's not perfect. It blurs the line between work and home. That's why Australia introduced the 'Right to Disconnect' legislation in 2024—employees don't need to respond outside work hours.

There's also a proximity bias. People in the office may have more visibility and opportunity. And most leaders still haven't been trained in managing remote or hybrid teams—PwC Australia found less than a third have.

Hybrid work has significantly shifted how teams operate, and with that, team dynamics.

Common ongoing challenges include: communication, collaboration, fewer informal interactions, digital fatigue, and barriers to building trust remotely.

A global study investigating the team dynamics and performance by remote work found that the biggest factors impacting remote team dynamics are:

- Goal clarity and alignment.
- Leadership style.
- Team structure and composition.
- Communication norms and expectations.
- Communication tools and technology.
- Trust and relationship building.

But hybrid also unlocks opportunity—access to talent, saved commuting time, and better work-life balance. If the office is for collaboration, design the environment that way: for connection, expanding networks, sharing knowledge, brainstorming, learning, and celebrating successes (McKinsey's *The Future of the Office Report*). Be intentional. Don't let connection happen by accident. Identify the *moments that matter*—why and when people come in. Co-create your team's flexible work approach.

Hybrid amplifies subcultures—different people, days, and locations mean different experiences. Corridor conversations matter. How can you intentionally create informal conversations? Manage for outcomes, not hours. Trust and autonomy are critical.

🌐 REAL-WORLD CASE STUDY

Medibank's four-day work week

Medibank is a leading health insurer in Australia. Australia is experiencing a period of significant health transition and requires innovation. Medibank is responding to this challenge by transforming how they work.

In October 2023, Medibank launched a four-day work week. This trial was for 250 employees which was later expanded in late 2024 to 500 employees. The 100:80:100 model means that employees get 100% of their pay for 80% of their hours, with the expectation of 100% productivity. This is one of the largest trials of its kind in Australia.

Macquarie University is monitoring the trial and has found improvements in engagement, job satisfaction, absenteeism, intentions to leave, better work-life balance, and health (reduced stress, improved sleep, healthier habits, and increased exercise).

As Rebecca Mitchell, Professor and Director, HoWRU, Macquarie University, told Medibank: *"These findings affirm the transformative potential of the four-day working week experiment in fostering a healthier, more engaged, and more resilient workforce. The substantial reductions in job stress, turnover intentions, and work-to-family conflict, alongside improvements in physical health and workplace support, position Medibank as a leader in innovative work arrangements."*

Kylie Bishop, Group Lead – People, Spaces & Sustainability at Medibank, said on HRMOnline: *"Employees inherently understand what low-value work is, so instead of telling teams how to manage their time, it's about creating space for teams to manage their own schedules. Teams innovated by reducing unproductive work like unnecessary meetings, double handling, and duplication of reporting, and implementing efficient processes like asynchronous communication, templates, and purposeful workflows."*

From a team perspective, they eliminated low-value tasks, reduced unnecessary meetings, and streamlined communication; teams were more autonomous, and work was redesigned.

Traditional, hybrid, and remote teams can thrive. It's how they work and interact that matters most. Leaders need to be intentional, so teams are connected.

What thriving teams do differently:

- Co-create hybrid ways of working.
- Identify 'moments that matter' for in-person.
- Manage for outcomes, not hours.
- Build clarity around communication norms.
- Design rituals for connection.
- Train leaders to manage hybrid teams.

Hybrid work isn't the problem. The lack of intentionality is. Where teams work is less important than how teams work.

How teams work

We get caught up in the busyness cycle. But motion doesn't necessarily equal progress. We need to create space for deep, focused work that clearly links to the priorities of the team.

THOUGHT LEADER INSIGHTS

Reducing capacity erosion

Dermot Crowley is a productivity expert and author of four books: *Smart Work, Smart Teams, Lead Smart* and *Urgent!* When I spoke to Dermot on the *Thriving Leaders Podcast*, he explained that thriving teams reduce internal and external capacity erosion.

He said internal capacity erosion happens when individuals don't have good personal productivity systems in place. External erosion stems from how teams interact—creating productivity friction for each other with unnecessary meetings, poor communication, and unclear priorities.

"We individually need to understand how we contribute and take personal accountability and effort, as our individual efficiency impacts the team's efficiency. Teams can create immense noise for each other, whether that's unnecessary meetings, emails, information overload, or work that isn't aligned to the strategic direction.

Leaders can also create urgency by default based on their authority. This can cause overwhelm and confusion about what is most important. Leaders need to role model how they use and protect their time. If leaders don't step back to reflect on how they're working—and the culture they're creating—they'll continue to be the friction they're trying to remove."

Key learnings: Understand the internal and external capacity erosion within the team. Thriving teams build strong cultures around communication, meetings, and prioritisation.

Prioritisation

We often wear our busyness badge with honour. But the constantly crammed calendars, bouncing from meeting to meeting, and the pressure to multitask—these end up leading to not-so-great outcomes. The to-do list never ends. There are so many things to do that it can be hard to know where to start. We're all busy.

Prioritisation isn't about time—it's about choices. The challenge I see with many leadership teams is balancing business-as-usual (BAU) with strategic priorities. They're trying to work out whether they've got the resources and budget to deliver on both. It's full of trade-offs, so teams need to learn how to prioritise what truly matters.

When I work with leadership teams, we prioritise together—distinguishing BAU from strategic initiatives. This forces a conversation about resource allocation, budgets, operational efficiencies, and trade-offs—whether that's reducing low-impact BAU or deprioritising strategic initiatives. It requires managing conflicting priorities to create a clear action plan that integrates BAU and strategy.

In *The 7 Habits of Highly Effective People* and *First Things First*, Stephen Covey shares that we should strive for effectiveness over efficiency. That means focusing on what matters most—not just what's urgent. His thinking is based on the Eisenhower Matrix, which categorises tasks into four quadrants:

1. Urgent and important: Do it.
2. Not urgent but important: Plan it.
3. Urgent but not important: Delegate it.
4. Neither urgent nor important: Ditch it.

I encourage teams to use this model when they're stuck in reactive, fire-fighting mode. It helps reduce the feeling that *everything* is urgent and clarifies what genuinely deserves attention.

As a team, you might wish to map out your priorities and deprioritise others.

It doesn't matter how productive you are—there's no way to give every task the same level of energy and attention. You need to work out, both individually and collectively, where to focus your energy.

The Priority Matrix is a useful tool to understand the impact (value or benefit) vs the effort (resource, time, energy):

- Quick wins (high impact, low effort): Do these first.

- Major projects (high impact, high effort): Plan and schedule.
- Thankless tasks (low impact, high effort): Postpone.
- Fill-ins (low impact, low effort): Delete.

Use this matrix when you're sorting strategic priorities, project planning, or sequencing initiatives. I've used it with leadership teams alongside OKRs—especially when the team is juggling too many initiatives without the time, budget, or headcount to deliver them all.

Focus time

In today's modern workplaces we have created environments of busyness and overwhelm. Teams are under-resourced, and are asked to do more with less. Let alone the constant pings, emails, and digital noise.

Dr David Rock, neuroscientist and author of *How the Brain Works*, says that cognitive tasks use energy. Prioritisation, planning, and scheduling, including your to-do list, requires a lot of energy from your prefrontal cortex. This sets your day up when your energy is at its peak. Next, plan to work on your most important energy-consuming tasks when your energy is at its peak. Noting, the research is based on neurotypical brains.

In my first book *Thriving Leaders*, I discuss what a day at JVAT, a management consultancy that has built a productive rhythm for their people, looks like. They start the day by prioritising, which is when the team communicates daily goals. Next, the team carve out two to three hours each morning for focused time, where there are no meetings or distractions for uninterrupted deep work. In the afternoons, it's time to meet. This is supported by David Rock's work, as this is a lower cognitive demand.

Even writing this book reminded me how important deep work is. When I only had a couple of hours blocked out for writing, I'd just be getting into it, and then I'd have to stop. But when I blocked out whole days and held myself accountable, I could get into flow and produce my best work. The Pomodoro Technique has worked for me during deep work—25 minutes of focused effort, followed by a five-minute break. The break matters—stretch, grab a cuppa, go to the loo. Then reset.

I work from home when I'm not with clients—and literally while writing this paragraph, my son came in twice with random questions. I ended up showing him what I had just typed which was ... According to research from the University of California, it takes 23 minutes and 15 seconds to return to a state of flow when we are interrupted. I then heard him relaying this to his brother, who was approaching my office door.

Teams need to stop the interruption culture. Create boundaries and focus time. Teams need to protect these boundaries for deep work. Set standards and expectations, and be intentional with them. As Dermot Crowley says, "Make the exceptions exceptional."

Breaks and rest

Thriving teams are thoughtful about their priorities. They make space for deep work, focused time, and also take time to pause, have breaks, and recharge. Back-to-back meetings, instant messaging pings, and interruptions leave us overwhelmed and tired.

We often go from one meeting to the next without any breaks in between. *Slack's Workforce Index* of over 10,000 desk workers globally found that 50% don't take breaks throughout the workday. When they surveyed their teams internally, they found that only two in five employees felt comfortable taking breaks. So they ran an experiment to encourage team members to pause. Over 200 employees signed up to participate, where for two weeks they would receive daily prompts to take breaks. They were also surveyed to track the number and types of breaks, and to measure their productivity and wellbeing. The results showed:

- 21% increase in productivity.
- 73% increase in work-life balance.
- 230% (2.3×) increase in ability to manage stress.
- 92% increase in ability to focus on work.
- 63% increase in overall job satisfaction.

They are some pretty impressive results. Think it's time for a break right now ...

I'm back, just went for a walk in the sunshine and had lunch. Personally, taking breaks is something I have never been great at. Our team actively focuses on personal goals as well as work goals. This year I'm focusing on movement. Working from home often leads to hours-long sitting at a desk. Research shows that performing just 10 bodyweight squats every 45 minutes during an 8.5-hour sitting period can improve blood sugar regulation more effectively than a 30-minute walk. Even if you meet the weekly exercise guidelines, these benefits are neutralised when sitting for more than five hours (like I often do, apart from my cuppa tea, food, and bathroom breaks). To counter this, I've started habit stacking—doing squats or lunges while waiting for the kettle to boil or my teabag to seep.

Research also suggests that microbreaks, of less than 10 minutes, can recharge the brain. Fresh air, a short walk, stretch, or a healthy snack all help. Manage your energy. Be conscious of the meeting culture that is being created within your team. Create space between meetings, don't just push through. Break the one-hour meeting rhythm.

I've recently changed my meeting calendar times to 25 minutes, 40 minutes, and 55 minutes. This means that I have a five-minute break in between meetings, so I'm not in back-to-backs.

I'm definitely better at switching off on holidays than I am at taking regular breaks during the day—but I'm working on it. Ensure your team takes holidays and breaks.

Can you see how much better the last few paragraphs were after my break?!

Workflow

Communication

In my opinion, communication is the most important skill that any person on the planet can learn. Understanding each other's communication styles within the team is key—it gives us insight into how to work together more effectively. Are you clear on how and when you communicate? Be explicit about different communication channels. For example:

- Email for formal communication.
- Teams/Slack used for quick updates and informal chats.
- Meetings for discussion, decision, and connection.

Repetition of key messages is essential for effective communication in teams. People often need to hear things more than once, especially in busy environments.

Role model what the communication expectations are. Don't send emails late at night or use the 'send later' function, so you aren't setting the expectations that this is expected from others.

How do you create opportunities for collaboration and connection?

Transparency of work

Make work visible. Use workflow management tools like kanban boards so people know who is working on what. This can be a physical visual management board, or an online tool, so everyone has visibility about who is accountable for what. It is also a great way to understand workloads, resource allocation, priorities, duplication, and align on what really matters.

This allows teams to track progress, dependencies, and have discussions about blockers and derailers.

At Thriving Culture, we use Asana to manage our workflow. This is integrated into Teams and our CRM. We align our strategy with three OKRs and this is also monitored as projects in Asana along with separate boards for our BAU. We also manage our meeting agenda in here. If you use Microsoft tools, Planner and OneNote work well too.

Making work visible creates healthy peer pressure and accountability as a team. Self-reporting keeps you on track with what you need to focus on and provides autonomy. Use tools to document processes. Something as simple as recording a Loom video (with transcript) can be a great training tool for new team members.

Technology

The Australian Productivity Commission (2025) has endorsed working from home, but cited that the country's recent decline in productivity was due to an underinvestment in technology.

Utilise technology tools to facilitate collaboration, particularly for virtual meetings. Screen sharing, document sharing, virtual whiteboards, real-time polling help to engage team members in the discussion and ensure all voices are heard. Platforms now have

AI integrations that provide meeting notes and summaries and actions, which helps to streamline workflow.

Dashboards or performance metrics help track progress, support better decisions, and assist with resource allocation.

When I wrote my first book, Jo in my team would collate information on certain topics and bring together diverse research and viewpoints. Now I use Perplexity, an AI tool, as a research assistant. On a daily basis, our team use Large Language Models to streamline reporting, synthesise data, fact check information, research prospective clients, create templates, create new images for presentations, and review documents for spelling and grammar, that all would have taken hours. It has made us more efficient as a team. AI is advancing exponentially. By the time you read this, AI will have advanced even further.

Many studies show that teams that utilise AI outperform those that rely solely on human collaboration, in productivity, quality, and innovation.

Teams still require human skills to be high performing. And AI is forcing us to communicate more clearly. You can't be vague with AI—you need to have crystal clear and specific instructions about the outcome, and what success looks like. Clarity is critical for AI, as it is for our people.

THOUGHT LEADER INSIGHTS

Using Large Language Models (LLMs) in teams

On the *Thriving Leaders Podcast*, AI expert Justin Williams highlighted the benefits and risks of AI in teams—noting that LLMs are brilliant for speed and scale, but human judgement must be applied. But we can't ignore the risks. We also discussed how leaders and organisations need to manage these—from data privacy and IP leakage, to over-reliance on false facts, erosion of critical thinking, prompt bias, and even the environmental impact and potential geopolitical misuse. Here are Justin's thoughts:

"LLMs are sensational for being able to augment what people do and make things happen more quickly. It's presenting some great opportunities for spending our time on the higher-value tasks; 85% of it is really good, and it can produce that in time that humans cannot. But it's the last 15%, that critical thinking, that really requires human intelligence and the diligence to check it for accuracy, for context, and for utility.

I think about LLMs as another team member to augment that thinking. Teams can certainly lift their performance by assigning standard tasks to LLMs. When the grunt work drops away, we get to spend more time having quality conversations that really move the needle. LLMs are an asset—almost a co-participant in the meeting—enriching the discussion so we get there faster. Teams will thrive into the future, but they will thrive differently."

Key learnings: Use LLMs to speed the work and widen thinking, then make the human call—check the facts, mine the data, and keep team dialogue front and centre.

The biggest risk for thriving teams with AI that I see is that the team stops collaborating and asking questions. It takes vulnerability to say "Hey, I don't know. Can you help me out?", and when you have lots of answers at your fingertips, teams stop communicating and connecting. Linked to this is inter-team learning. Encourage connection and team learning.

Ensure that your team is technology-enabled to connect, communicate, and collaborate effectively.

Team principles

Co-create guiding principles of what you expect of each other as a team. Dermot Crowley calls them team agreements. Some teams call it a team charter or even the team playbook.

These are different from your team's purpose and values, but they should be used in conjunction with them.

- Your team **purpose** is why you exist as a team.
- Your **values** are the behaviours you demonstrate when you're together.
- Your **principles** are the expectations you hold of each other.

Let's be honest—some common meeting behaviours that aren't okay include:

- People working on other things during the meeting.
- Taking calls or texting mid-meeting.
- Having side conversations.
- Not speaking up at all (then debriefing afterwards in the 'real' meeting).
- One person hijacking the agenda or going off on tangents.
- Camera off, while they are multi-tasking.

Recognise any of these?

Dermot Crowley talks about the importance of meeting, communication, and prioritisation cultures within teams. I recommend developing **team principles** that fall into these three buckets:

1. Meeting
2. Communication
3. Prioritisation

Start by identifying team friction points, then agree on the behaviours or actions that will help you work better together. Here are some examples.

Meeting principles

These help teams meet with purpose and stop wasting time in unproductive gatherings.

Here are some example meeting principles:

- **Clear meeting purpose:** We don't meet for the sake of it.
- **Rotate the chair:** Share the load of meeting chair; use the agreed agenda but bring your own flair.
- **Meeting observer:** Nominate someone to assess how effective the meeting was. Did we live our values and purpose? Rotate this role.
- **Protect focus time:** No meetings between 8.30–10.30 a.m. Block it out. Defend it.
- **Start and end on time:** All team meetings begin at five past and finish at five to.
- **Respect time zones:** For global teams, double-check before you send that 6 a.m. calendar invite.
- **Come prepared:** Pre-reads go out two days before. Read them before showing up.
- **Cameras on, present and focused:** Show up like it's in person. Set yourself to 'Do Not Disturb' in virtual meetings. No checking phones or taking other calls.

Communication principles

These create clarity, build trust, and help us deal with issues early— before they become big.

Here are some example communication principles:

- **Use the right channel to communicate**:
  - Email = formal.
  - Teams = quick, informal communications.
  - Calls = urgency or connection.
  - Meetings = collaboration and decisions.
- **Respect response times and boundaries:** Agree on tool use and don't expect a response outside of business hours.
- **CC = FYI only:** Don't expect a reply if you're just looping someone in.
- **Silence = Agreement:** If you don't speak up, we assume you agree. No meetings after the meeting.
- **Feedback is frequent and welcome:** It's two-way, timely, and focused on learning, not judgement.
- **Celebrate and acknowledge:** Show gratitude. Recognise contributions and strengths.
- **Respect diversity of thought:** Curiosity over judgement. Ask questions. Actively listen. Make space for all voices.
- **Communicate with the right people:** Be intentional about who's included in conversations and decisions.

Prioritisation principles

These help the team stay aligned, manage overwhelm, and focus on impact.

Here are some example prioritisation principles:

- **We focus on what matters:** Prioritise by impact and effort, not urgency or noise.
- **We align before we act:** For team priorities, we get on the same page first.

- **We adapt when things shift:** If priorities change, we communicate them.
- **We track progress transparently:** Dashboards are live and visible.
- **We have permission to say no:** If we've agreed something's not worth doing, drop it.
- **BAU doesn't excuse ignoring strategy:** We balance today's tasks with tomorrow's goals.
- **We check for duplication:** We question to ensure no double handling.
- **We challenge respectfully:** We question priorities to ensure it will enable strategy.

Start with meeting and communication principles—get those humming before you add prioritisation. Don't over-engineer this. You don't need a laundry list—just the essentials that will help your team perform at its best.

Building a thriving team is an ongoing practice—it's not a 'set and forget'. Things go off-track (especially during high-stress periods). What matters is having the rhythm and reflection points to get back on track.

Connection

Connection isn't just about being in the same room—it's how we stay aligned, engaged, and human while getting the work done. Thriving teams are intentional about how they connect, no matter where they work. They create rhythms and rituals, build trust, and have clear processes that bring clarity and cohesion.

Whether it's sharing stories, setting better meeting habits, or carving out time for deep work, connection is the groove that keeps the team in sync. It's emotional, it's practical, and it's powerful.

Connection doesn't happen by chance. It's created, nurtured, and protected—especially in the messy, hybrid, high-pressure reality of today's workplaces.

How connected is your team ... really?

What thriving teams do differently:

- Get to know each other beyond the work.
- Have simple team processes and ways of working.
- Create team principles, habits and rituals.

Actions

1. **Get to know each other beyond the work.** Create opportunities for connection. Build this into your operating rhythm, formally and informally. Be intentional. Encourage social connection and for team members to be their authentic selves.

2. **Create team habits and rituals.** Build the team culture and bind the team together. Celebrate success, recognise both the small and large achievements of your team.

3. **Define and review your operating rhythm.** Have clear team meeting cadence, frequency, purpose, and agendas. Set up one-on-one meetings. Tailor the frequency based on individual needs to discuss performance and development.

4. **Co-create team principles.** Get the team involved in creating the Meeting, Communication, and Prioritisation Principles.

5. **Promote transparency and visibility.** Create clear job descriptions and workflow tools to track accountability and workload.

RESOURCES

www.thrivingculture.com.au/ttbook

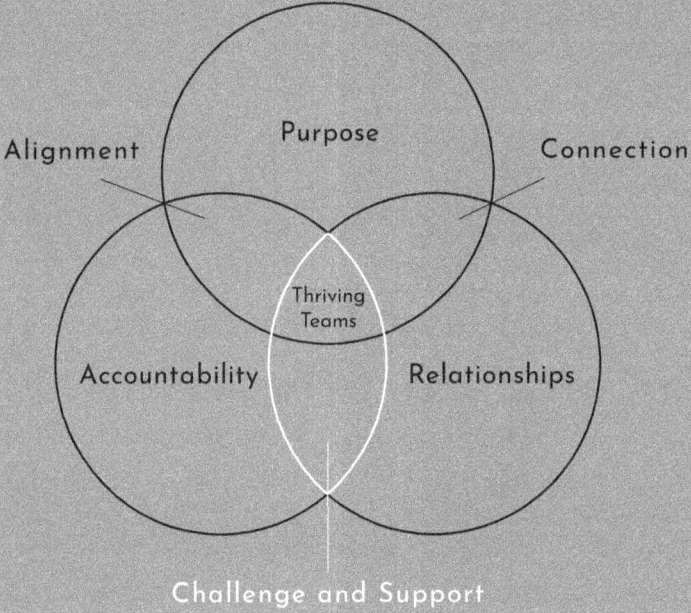

Alignment

Purpose

Connection

Thriving
Teams

Accountability

Relationships

Challenge and Support

Thriving teams strike a healthy balance, challenge one another to be at their best, support each other, have each other's backs, and learn from one another. They aren't nice or passive. They have healthy, challenging debates and get everything out on the table that needs to be said for the greater good of the team. When they challenge each other to think differently and expand their ideas, the team grows.

Teams learn just like individuals do. They learn from their mistakes, failures, and successes. They ask for help when they are struggling or risk missing a deadline. They don't feel judged for doing so.

In the Thriving Teams Model, Challenge and Support sit between Relationships (which includes psychological safety and trust) and Accountability. Getting this balance right is critical.

We need to get the balance right between being assertive and empathetic. It's the tension between accountability (challenge) and relationships (support). We work best when there is this productive tension.

Amy Edmondson in her book *The Fearless Organisation* shares a powerful 2×2 matrix. This matrix looks at challenge (accountability) and support (psychological safety):

- **Apathy zone:** Low support and low challenge. People are detached, they don't really care about their work, they do the bare minimum for self-protection.
- **Anxiety Zone:** Low support and high challenge. People hold back, are reluctant to take risks or offer ideas out of fear. The pressure is high and demands may feel unreasonable.
- **Comfort Zone:** High support and low challenge. People feel safe to share their ideas; however, they don't take ownership for performance standards.

- **Learning Zone:** High support and high challenge. People collaborate, learn from mistakes, share ideas, and hold each other accountable.

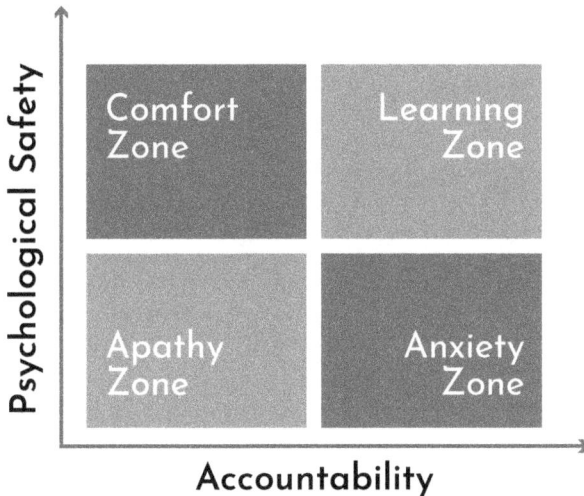

The learning zone is what we are striving for as a thriving team. McKinsey's found that only 26% of teams are in the learning zone with challenge and support present.

So why do we find it so hard to challenge each other at work? Because it feels risky. We don't want to upset people, or rock the boat, or come across as difficult. But challenge, done well, isn't about being difficult. It's about caring enough to say the thing that needs to be said—and creating an environment where it's safe to say it.

In this part we discuss Challenge and Support, by unpacking healthy debate and learning.

CHAPTER 10

Healthy Debate

*Honest disagreement is often
a good sign of progress.*
— Mahatma Gandhi

Thriving teams have healthy, challenging debates. Meetings are lively and passionate. There is disagreement, challenge, and a pursuit for what is best for the team or organisation. The balance of psychological safety and accountability means that teams can have robust conversations without agendas, egos, or politics getting in the way.

Nice teams often mask fear with a layer of politeness. On the opposite end are teams that argue just to push their own agenda, where the loudest voice wins.

> ### 💡 THOUGHT LEADER INSIGHTS
>
> **High-quality conversations**
> Most teams talk a lot but don't always learn together—Amy Edmondson argues the sweet spot is high standards with high psychological safety so people feel supported emotionally and challenged intellectually. Leaders should treat dialogue like a

core skill: design conversations where people share what they know, listen hard, ask real questions and include every voice.

Here is what Amy shared on the *Thriving Leaders Podcast*.

"You need the heat and the heart. The work is meaningful and hard, but I'm not so worried about self-protection that it distracts me from the work. We've been trained in impression management. From school through to career, we learn to look good, not to learn. And that's unhelpful in an uncertain world. We need to unlearn the highly skilled behaviour of looking good and relearn the behaviour of learning in teams with each other.

These conversations are rare and skilful. And most people haven't been trained in the skills of high-quality conversation. High-quality conversations have three attributes: people are sharing what they know and listening intently; there's a healthy mix of questions and statements; and there's a sense of making progress.

We're all participants and assessors. If someone is quiet, we invite them in. If someone's dominating, we balance the conversation. Everyone has the potential and the invitation to improve the quality of dialogue. The quality of our conversations is a very real responsibility, especially in leadership teams.

High-quality conversations are ones where people aren't holding back—the truth, their ideas, or their reactions to each other's ideas. They're doing their best to express themselves thoughtfully and skilfully—not with anger or blame, but with intention and care.

These conversations also include a healthy mix of idea sharing, experience sharing, and high-quality questions—questions that draw out each other's knowledge.

And importantly, there's a sense of progress. You feel like we're getting somewhere. I'm getting smarter. You're getting smarter. We're moving toward resolving the issue at hand.

Conversations with those three attributes are rare. They're skilful. But when you lean into building those kinds of conversations, you're leaning into building psychological safety."

Key learnings: Set the intention and build the skill for high-quality conversations in your team.

Conflict and not making things personal

When some people hear the word conflict, they immediately constrict. They might get defensive, aggressive, or even withdraw. Patrick Lencioni talks about engaging in unfiltered conflict. I call it healthy debate.

Most people avoid conflict because of the discomfort that comes with it. Depending on your natural personality style, people will have different levels of comfort with conflict. Some people avoid it at all costs. For others, they have learnt the skills to feel confident to have difficult conversations, but on the inside, the discomfort they feel is very real. Then there are others who love going head-to-head.

Gender can also influence how we approach conflict. Women tend to be more relational and willing to name the unspoken. Men are often more task-focused or withdraw to preserve status (Cinardo, 2011). In many leadership teams, I've noticed women are more likely to say: "We probably should name the elephant in the room." But they're also less likely to speak up if the environment isn't psychologically safe.

Cultural differences also play a role. In *The Culture Map*, Erin Meyer, professor of management practice at INSEAD, one of the world's leading international business schools, explains that some cultures—like the Dutch—are comfortable with open disagreement and direct feedback. Others—like Japan—prefer subtle disagreement to preserve group harmony. As leaders, we need to make explicit how our team debates and resolves issues. And be careful not to overemphasise differences—this can lead to stereotyping (Livermore, 2025).

⚙ **TEAM IN PRACTICE**

Silent team members

In a global logistics company, the senior operations team met regularly to address supply chain challenges across regions. But in those meetings, only a handful of voices were heard. The extroverts dominated discussions, while quieter members—often from different cultural or functional backgrounds—remained silent. On paper the team looked diverse, but in practice, only a fraction of perspectives were being heard.

The imbalance grew over time. The quieter team members began to disengage, assuming their input wasn't valued. They contributed less and less, which only reinforced the dominance of the louder voices. As a result, the team missed opportunities to surface new ideas and approaches, and innovation suffered.

The Regional Director leading the team described it like this:

- "It feels like only half the room is in the conversation."
- "Some of our best thinkers aren't being heard."
- "We're losing out on the diversity we actually have."

To shift the dynamic, the leader introduced new ways of running meetings—rotating who chaired discussions, building in structured rounds for input, and actively drawing in the quieter members. Over time, this created a more inclusive environment where every perspective was valued. The change unlocked richer problem-solving and helped the team make faster decisions in a highly complex operating environment.

Task conflict vs relationship conflict

Task conflict arises when team members have different views about the work. For example, a salesperson chasing individual sales targets may do so at the expense of the account management team, who then struggle to service that client due to capacity issues.

Relationship conflict is more personal—it's a perceived inter-personal difference. Left unaddressed, task conflict can escalate into relationship conflict. The account manager now assumes the sales-person only cares about commission—it's no longer about the work, it's personal.

Bring it back to the work. Don't personalise or play the blame game. What's the challenge, issue, or opportunity to solve? Can we see multiple perspectives? Embrace task conflict by debating ideas, challenging assumptions, and being open to other viewpoints. Healthy conflict is honest, open, and goal-focused—it improves performance.

Being nice can lead to passive behaviours

There is a common misconception that a psychologically safe team is a nice team. Nice teams avoid conflict to preserve relationships. Team silence is a shared issue. Even if it is just one person staying silent, voices aren't being heard. Silence does not equal agreement. If people don't feel safe to speak up, psychological safety isn't present in the environment.

The unintended consequence of a performance culture is the erosion of psychological safety. NASA, a commonly cited example, after the *Challenger* (1986) and *Columbia* (2003) disasters, found that their performance culture stopped people from challenging assumptions. Groupthink, fear of speaking up as their expertise wouldn't be valued, and pressure to conform, meant team members stayed silent—despite having concerns.

After the shuttle disasters, NASA's investigations found they needed a learning culture. They improved communication and introduced an environment where concerns could be raised freely by anyone, regardless of their position, so that critical decision-makers were informed and accountable for safety decisions.

Fear

Passive behaviours can lead to passive aggression. Withdrawing, the silent treatment, withholding information, agreeing in the meeting but not following through, turning up late, excluding others, sarcasm—these all send a message.

This behaviour often stems from a fear. One of my favourite models is the SCARF model by David Rock, which explains the social threats people experience. Often with executive coaching clients, they become perplexed by another colleague's behaviour. When we unpack the behaviour, we often uncover a social threat that that colleague may be experiencing. This then informs the approach to take with that individual. These include:

- **Status:** Our relative importance to others (remind them they're valued, acknowledge their expertise).
- **Certainty:** Our ability to predict the future (share what you know and what's coming, be clear with expectations).
- **Autonomy:** Our sense of control over events (let them own what they can, give them choices).
- **Relatedness:** How safe we feel with others (keep them connected, show you care, and role model vulnerability).
- **Fairness:** How just we perceive exchanges between people (be transparent in the precedents that are being set).

If a relationship is strained, take some accountability for your part. Reflect before reacting. Put yourself in their shoes to unpack what the real issue is. Notice your emotional reaction to the situation and how that influences the dynamics.

Debating, healthy debate

I've always used the term 'healthy debate' with teams. When David Clutterbuck came on the *Thriving Leaders Podcast*, he challenged me on this language.

"When you have a debate, somebody's trying to win an argument—that's not that healthy," he said. "When you have discussion, you're trying to find a compromise. When you have dialogue, you're trying to find new meaning, new ways forward. Dialogue is where you are exploring ideas, you're putting ideas out there to be challenged—and for you to challenge your own thinking as well. At the end of a significant meeting, say: 'What needed to be said but wasn't said?'"

I've grappled with this since. The word debate can bring flashbacks to high school debating teams—rigid rebuttals and winning or losing. Or worse, parliamentary-style yelling matches.

But not all debate is like that.

In Tibetan Buddhism, debate is a philosophical enquiry and a wisdom tradition. A daily theatrical practice in that tradition involves a challenger who stands, claps, and provokes, and the responder who sits, grounded, and answers. They switch roles regularly to debate Buddhist philosophy. They learn to hold tension, ask sharp questions, and uncover the complexity of truth. Debate is about mutual learning to sharpen shared understanding and collective insight. Their focus is on ideas, not individuals or winning. It exposes misconceptions, tests assumptions and defensible viewpoints.

We should leverage the philosophy of Tibetan Buddhist debate in the corporate world. Healthy debate in a team is what is needed. Healthy debate is where we share different perspectives, listen to each other, respectfully disagree, and generate better ideas together as a team to then arrive at a solution. It isn't about the person, it's about the challenge. We don't want teams to agree; we want disagreement, as it leads to innovation.

The irony of me debating the word debate is not lost on me! Having a different view from someone I respect, admire, and have studied under further demonstrates the point that we don't always need to agree to learn from each other.

Create a holding environment to turn up the heat

In June 2024, I went to Harvard Kennedy School for a week-long executive immersive experience called the 'Art and Practice of Leadership Development'. Here we were learning about leadership expert Ronald Heifetz and Marty Linksy's Adaptive Leadership Framework. Adaptive leadership is the practice of mobilising people to tackle tough challenges, adapt, and thrive.

This was one of the most challenging weeks of my life. It pushed me into discomfort in the service of learning. The combination of jet lag, confusion, tension, and overthinking added to the richness of the learning. The facilitators—Ron Heifetz along with other Harvard Kennedy faculty members Tim O'Brien and Farayi Chipungu—created a powerful 'holding environment'. They did this by using what is called Case-In-Point. This is an immersive experiential methodology, where the people in the room represent the system and what you are learning in real time in the room.

A holding environment is a safe space for groups to experience discomfort, uncertainty, and tension. Even with 63 people from 19 countries in the room, they managed to build a space for deep contemplation, courageous dialogue, and collective learning.

A holding environment is required to get to the 'productive zone of disequilibrium' with teams. When there is not enough heat, we get complacent and avoidant. Too much heat can burn us out, or we become reactive. When the heat's too high or the environment isn't safe, people experience social threats. The brain goes into protection mode—defensiveness, withdrawal, or shutdown.

Teams need to get comfortable with the discomfort. Change is messy. It disrupts the status quo. There's loss and frustration. But growth never comes from staying the same. Leaders need to push the learning threshold and move into the productive zone. When we get the balance right, the magic happens.

Leaders need to regulate the heat, to push just enough to stretch but not snap. Turning up the heat might mean increasing urgency, surfacing an unspoken issue, or asking a bigger question. It forces a different kind of conversation. It sparks creativity and problem-solving. And yes, it might get uncomfortable. That's the point.

As the leader, it's your job to create that holding environment—a container where challenge can happen, and growth can follow. This environment has psychological safety and accountability.

The healthy debate model

Leaders need to create the environment, give permission, and set boundaries for healthy debate.

Use the Healthy Debate Model and build it into your team's DNA.

There are four steps to creating healthy debate within your team. These are:

1. **Diagnose:** Get clear on the real problem. Get on the balcony, look at the system, and consider multiple interpretations.

2. **Dialogue:** Create the conditions for generative dialogue. Listen to learn, ask curious questions, and share perspectives.
3. **Decide:** Be clear on how decisions are made as a team. Play back what was decided and agree next steps.
4. **Dedicate:** Show a united front and communicate with one aligned voice. Commit to the way forward.

Diagnose

Teams can often skip the diagnosis part and proceed directly to debating a topic. This is an important first step to ensure that you are focusing on the right problem that needs to be solved. Some teams are quick to move to solution mode. When teams do this, they risk solving the wrong problem. There are often assumptions that are driving the conversation. There are teams that love a good talk fest. They have circular conversations sharing their points of view. They talk in circles, but no decisions are made.

Start by defining the problem, goal, or decision that needs to be addressed. This could be as simple as creating a problem statement or articulating the goal or outcome to achieve. This ensures that everyone is on the same page. Gather data to ensure the team has the facts. This helps us not jump to conclusions. Identify any assumptions or biases the team holds.

For simple problems, use the 5 Whys technique to get to the root cause of an issue. Ask 'why' five times through iterative questioning. Then ask one 'how' to identify what's next. This doesn't work for more complex or systemic issues.

Adaptive challenges are complex; they require listening and feedback loops, as well as observing and interpreting the situation. We must learn the way forward and make decisions based on our interpretations. The adaptive leadership framework encourages us to stay in diagnosis. Teams need to 'get on the balcony' to understand what's really going on. We take a broader perspective, look at the system, and make strategic observations. The 'dance floor' is when we are immersed in action. We are in the situation or challenge and we focus on what's directly in front of us. We need to move between both. Generate multiple hypotheses and perspectives to challenge your assumptions—observe and interpret.

Dialogue

Dialogue is a way that we develop shared meaning, we build on each other's ideas, generate new ideas, challenge the status quo, hold our views lightly, speak up without being judged, and collaborate. This is where we want to hear from all the voices in the room. To get all the different perspectives on the table and look at things from different angles.

Provide positive feedback to those who share bold ideas, different points of view, and speak up. Healthy debate helps us challenge our thinking, innovate, appreciate diversity of thought with ultimate outcome to improve our performance and goals. When teams are thriving, decisions are made in service of the team rather than your own agenda or ego.

At the core of any good conversation are three core elements:

1. **Listen to learn:** Actively listen. Be open to other perspectives, challenge assumptions.
2. **Ask curious questions:** Draw out knowledge and perspectives through thoughtful questioning.
3. **Share your perspective:** Express your knowledge and views. Don't hold back.

Listen to learn

> *Stop, collaborate and listen.*
>
> — Vanilla Ice

When we feel like someone is truly listening to us, we feel seen, valued, and heard. It is a fundamental skill to effective communication but one that often gets missed in teams.

Why is it so hard to listen? Our brains process words four times faster than someone can speak. The person listening will process what they are hearing with 25% of their mental capacity (Brownell, 2012). This means that 75% of our mental capacity is free to make judgements, have emotional reactions, for our mind to wander, multitask, think about something else, and get distracted. This cognitive overload impacts our attention. We also live in an age of digital distractions and noise. We need to minimise these distractions, especially when we are together as a team, so we can be fully present.

When we listen to learn, we are actively listening. We are fully present with the person speaking. We suspend judgement to truly understand what is being said. Active listening requires intentionality and presence. It also requires a level of self-awareness—managing our emotional responses and observing the cues presented by the person speaking.

The purpose of listening is to take in what the other person is saying—and what they're not saying. We go beyond the words. We draw meaning, emotion, and even insight from what's unsaid. We do this by tuning into how something is said—through tone, pace, and body language. Are they lively and excited? Frustrated and annoyed? When we're actively listening, we use that spare 75% of mental capacity to draw out the real meaning behind the message. This is the basis of emotional intelligence.

At Harvard, we did a powerful exercise called 'The Music Beneath the Words'. I read the poem my aunt read at my dad's funeral. When I read it aloud, making every word count with intention, my partner and I were in tears. It wasn't the words—it was the meaning behind them that landed. That's what listening with presence does.

Signs you are listening? You can paraphrase what someone said. You pick up on their language. You don't interrupt. You're not trying to fix or solve—you're just there with them. There are cues that show you are listening such as nodding and body language; however, we can get in our heads about showing we are listening, and stop focusing on what the person is saying.

At home, we tell our boys to listen with their eyes and ears. Sounds simple. But in teams, it's the same. You show you're listening by *actually* listening. Focus on being present and interested in what the person is saying. Make an intentional choice to listen fully.

One of my worst habits is finishing people's sentences. I tell myself I'm just excited—but it signals that I don't value what they're saying. I'm working on it. Listening to learn means hearing the full thought, without jumping in. Use the acronym WAIT: *Why Am I Talking?* Say it in your head. It gives space to others.

The best listeners aren't silent—they're present. Thriving teams that listen build on others' ideas, provide their perspectives, and are open to changing their view. They ask great questions and stay curious.

Ask curious questions

Our brains are hardwired to believe we're right. But the need to be right—or to make someone else wrong—can destroy relationships. Often, there is no single 'right' answer. We need to let go of ego and righteousness. If we hold the view that we are right, we are unlikely to be open to other perspectives.

People tend to become more defensive about *why* you're saying something than *what* you're saying. Defensiveness is one of the strongest predictors of relationship breakdown. It's often a form of self-protection when we feel criticised. When we remove judgement from our tone of voice, our message lands more clearly—and more kindly.

Coming from a place of curiosity is a skill that all team members must adopt. When we're curious, we dig deeper, don't take things at face value, and stay open to learning and hearing what is really being said.

Jeff Wetzler's Curiosity Curve is designed to gauge your initial mindset when walking into a conversation (Wetzler, 2025). When we are aware of our pattern of thinking, we can become more self-aware if it needs to shift.

The curiosity curve is a qualitative mental model, mapping various mindsets on a continuum, from zones of certainty through to zones of curiosity.

Zones of certainty:

- **Self-righteous disdain:** "I can't stand them."
- **Confident dismissal:** "I'm right."
- **Sceptical tolerance:** "I think they're wrong, but I'll hear them out."

Zones of curiosity:

- **Cautious openness:** "They could know something worth finding out."
- **Genuine interest:** "I truly understand their views and experience."
- **Fascinated wonder:** "There's so much I want to learn—from, with, and about them."

The next time you walk into a conversation, observe where your mindset is and set an intention. What mindset would you like to adopt? Think of curious questions you can ask to make the shift. Curiosity is a choice.

This means asking more open-ended 'what' and 'how' questions, which helps others explore their thinking. It unpacks other team members' pressures, helps them to explore meanings they may not have thought of, and presents new information and perspectives to the team.

When taking a coaching approach, imagine a funnel. Start with broad, open questions, then move on to clarifying questions, and finally, transition to more specific questions. Otherwise, we are likely to ask many leading questions that are actually suggestions masked as questions. Curious questions draw out knowledge and diverse thinking.

Leaders should be actively coaching the team. Coaching pioneer Sir John Whitmore's GROW model is a useful tool for teams to practise coaching each other when they are together.

- **Goal:** What do we want to achieve?
- **Reality:** What's the current situation?
- **Options:** What options are there?
- **Way forward:** What action will we take?

For more information on GROW and detailed questions, check out Chapter 4 – Coaching, in *Thriving Leaders*.

In your team, promote discussions based on curiosity, such as:

- How might we ...?
- What if ...?
- What can we learn from ...?

All great innovations have come from curiosity. It deepens thinking, triggers creativity, and forces collaboration. As the leader, coach your team explicitly—and build a culture where they coach each other too. If this is a skill that the team struggles with, bring in team coaches to help develop this capability within the team.

As David Clutterbuck says: "Finding answers is easy. Finding the right question is much harder."

Share perspectives

When I work with leadership teams, the thing they're most proud of is usually the expertise in the room. That's something to leverage. Thriving teams share their ideas, advocate for what they believe in, and contribute diverse perspectives. We want team members to share all the available information they have that is relevant to the current discussion.

Organisational psychologist Adam Grant, in *Think Again*, challenges us to unlearn and rethink what we believe to be true. Thriving teams embrace this mindset. They're open to being persuaded. They influence others by being curious and reflective, not just by holding strong views. Give people time to form their views—gather evidence, speak to stakeholders, and bring considered thinking to the table.

🌐 REAL-WORLD CASE STUDY

Shifting from an agreeable team

As Hive Legal evolved, the leadership team realised that their strength in relationships—while foundational—was unintentionally limiting their ability to challenge each other. A 360-degree review and personality profiling revealed that their leadership style, while high on trust and cohesion, was lower on challenge.

The shift focused on leaning into hard conversations and making accountability transparent.

As Principal Joanna Green shared: *"We've worked together for so long that it can be easy to avoid hard conversations. But we've had to learn to lean into disagreement, even when it's awkward—we were prioritising getting along. We started creating more space for respectful challenge. We're still a democracy—decisions are made collectively—but now we give people time to ask questions, reflect, and disagree. There's a high level of psychological safety and transparency in how we operate.*

People feel safe to say, 'I don't agree' or 'I'm uncomfortable with this' and we trust that the motivation is always to do what's best for the business. That openness has strengthened how we work and lifted performance across the board.

Something we've really focused on in recent years is leaning into the hard conversations. When things get tough, it's tempting to want to walk away or chase the next shiny thing. But there's so much value in having open, respectful dialogue—especially when you're part of a team that's thriving overall. Feedback often brings up things you had no idea someone was feeling or experiencing until they say it out loud. And yes, sometimes it's hard to hear. But it's incredibly useful. And if it doesn't come naturally, learn the skill. It's worth it if you're in it for the long haul."

When things get tough, people are tempted to bail. Hive's leaders do the opposite—they stay in the room and have open, respectful conversations. With the firm's size and flat leadership model, everything's visible—there's nowhere to hide—which strengthens trust and keeps accountability real.

As Executive Director and Experience Designer Melissa Lyon added: *"We expect people in our leadership team to be vulnerable, so that we can help. Sometimes, especially in the legal ecosystem, there is almost a deterrent to show weakness*

> *or vulnerability at a leadership level, because you should have that mask of 'I'm totally in control and I know what's happening.' Whereas as a team, we embrace it and support each other through those times as well."*
>
> If you are part of a team that always agrees, this may not be a good thing. When we always agree, there is a lot of groupthink and we are lacking diversity of thought.

We want teams to disagree. If your team always agrees, chances are you're slipping into complacency or groupthink. I'm not talking about disagreeing for the sake of it but genuinely seeking different perspectives.

A helpful metaphor comes from *You're It: Crisis, Change, and How to Lead When it Matters Most* by Marcus et al. The authors share the story of the 'Cone in the Cube'. This is an opaque cube; inside the cube is a cone. Two groups of people are asked to look inside the cube and decide what shape is inside. Group A looks through peephole A on the side of the cube, and they see a triangle. Group B looks through peephole B, and they see a circle. Understandably, both groups argue based on what they see, their own perspective. This leads to conflict and misunderstanding as they hold their own interpretation as the only perspective. We can often look at the same situation and have different observations. When we hold our own views so firmly, thinking we are right, it leads to conflict. When we can hold multiple perspectives at once, we unlock wider information and build a bigger-picture understanding. Holding rigid viewpoints can blind us.

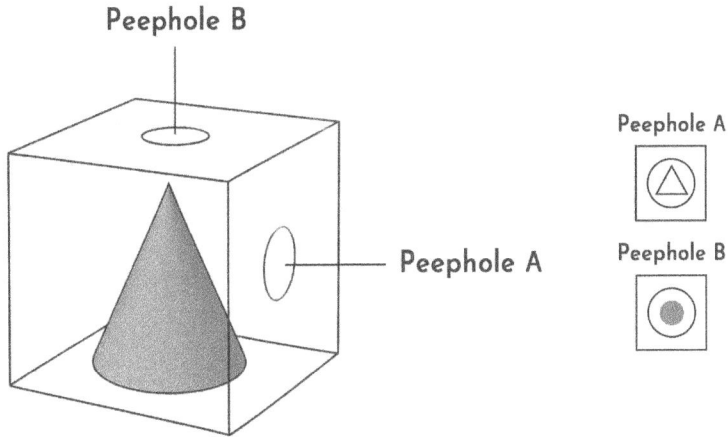

Peephole B

Peephole A

Peephole A

Peephole B

You can widen your perspective by bringing in voices from outside your team. When I facilitated a 2030 strategy session for a global insurance company client, we invited not just the Executive Team, but a handful of high-potential talent from different levels of the business, and stakeholders from across the world. It brought fresh thinking and future-focused insights.

If your team finds disagreement uncomfortable, reframe it as a positive. Try asking:

- What's been left unsaid?
- What's a perspective we haven't considered?
- What might we be avoiding?
- What's another interpretation?

Give permission to challenge ideas. Encourage constructive tension. Innovation lives there.

Not sure where to start? Practise debate in a low-stakes, playful way. Try topics like:

- Dogs vs cats?
- Butter under your peanut butter—yes or no?
- Pineapple on pizza?

Make it light, but passionate. Focus on the issue. Help the team build the muscles of disagreement, active listening, and perspective-taking.

One simple technique I love: ask team members with opposing views to articulate the other's position *in the first person*. This builds empathy, understanding, and a stronger collective voice.

If you don't share, your teammates will feel that you are holding back. Share your perspective. Be courageous and share your views with the team; don't hold back.

Decide

Making decisions as a team can feel tough. You've done the work, explored options and possible solutions. Debated, challenged, and remained curious. Now it's time to reach a decision. The team needs to align on a way forward.

Teams don't need to agree; they need to align.

Evidence-based decision-making is the ideal. The reality is that there is always an emotional element to decision-making. We also carry cognitive biases that sway how we perceive the world. Watch out for common team biases:

- **Authority bias:** Defaulting to the most senior person in the room when making a decision or not challenging their thinking.
- **Confirmation bias:** Highlighting information that validates our existing view, beliefs, or decisions, and discounting information that doesn't support our existing view.
- **Conformity bias:** We agree with others to fit in, leading to groupthink, focusing on consensus and harmony, suppressing dissent, and differing opinions.

- **Overconfidence bias:** Also known as the Dunning-Kruger Effect, where we overestimate our abilities, knowledge, and experience in an area. In teams, where someone is an expert, they may assume others have the same skill level as they do.
- **In-group/out-group bias:** We favour ideas or people that feel familiar, and discount those who feel different.
- **Sunk-cost trap:** Keep on going because of the past investment of time, money, or energy, rather than calling it.

Being aware of biases doesn't necessarily eliminate them within the team. Asking curious questions can help with this. It requires conscious effort. Always look at problems from multiple perspectives, seek diverse inputs from different people or styles within the team. Rotate devil's advocate for decisions in meetings to ensure that dissenting opinions are heard.

If LLMs are an extension of our team, we need to be mindful of the inherent biases that the algorithms contain; these blind spots can skew decisions.

There are so many decision-making models and thinking styles out there, from De Bono's *Six Thinking Hats*, Kahneman's *Thinking, Fast and Slow*, Chris Argyris's 'ladder of inference', Dave Snowden's 'Cynefin Framework', and Joy Paul Guilford's twin concepts of convergent thinking and divergent thinking, to name a few. I encourage you to check these out.

Anchor decisions to guiding principles, strategy, values, or the outcomes you have committed to. If your team is stuck in a stalemate, find the points of intersection that you can all agree on. Once that common ground is established, move from there. Often narrowing down your options and choices can help with making decisions. Give the team a decision deadline, if they have a tendency to talk in circles.

Understanding the stakes of a decision is important. For high-stakes decisions, there are bigger risks. Can we reverse this decision? Some decisions are reversible, some aren't. We need to balance the risks.

These conversations should feel like there is a sense of progress.

- What if we did nothing? Taking no action is an action.
- What's the cost of waiting?
- What have we missed or not considered?

Former editor-in-chief of the *Harvard Business Review* Suzy Welch's 10-10-10 method is a useful decision-making lens:

- What will the impact of this decision be in 10 minutes? (immediate)
- In 10 months? (medium term)
- In 10 years? (long term)

How does your team make decisions? Do they default to the most senior person in the room? Does the team talk in circles and not make progress? Does the team agree when together, then do their own things afterwards?

There is a difference between agreement and alignment. Teams don't need to agree, they need to align to the way forward.

Once a decision is made, lock it in. Play back what was decided—don't assume alignment, confirm it. Agree on next steps—who is doing what and by when.

Clarity + commitment = alignment

💡 THOUGHT LEADER INSIGHTS

David Clutterbuck on decision-making in teams

On the *Thriving Leaders Podcast*, David Clutterbuck shared a simple yet effective framework for decision-making in a team. Consensus can sometimes mean 'begrudging' acceptance—going along but not fully on board. What matters more is whether the team has true alignment. That's when you know you've got commitment, not just compliance.

"We've got hundreds, probably thousands of teams around the world using a simple yet powerful tool that starts with three reflective questions:

- *What do I want to say about this issue?*
- *What do I want to hear other people say about this issue?*
- *What do I want the outcome of the conversation to be?*

Each person writes down their answers. Then, one by one, each team member shares what they've written—without discussion, just clarification if needed. The team leader goes last. Only then does the actual discussion begin.

Three things consistently happen: 'It takes half as long' because everyone already knows where each other stands. The conversation becomes 'much more polite'—people listen better and refer back to others' concerns.

Consensus naturally emerges, or if the team leader needs to decide, they do so with clear rationale: 'I listened to all of these things, and I think I've got to go with this.'

The leader then checks:

- *Have you said what you needed to say?*
- *Have you heard what you needed to hear?*
- *Have you achieved what you needed to achieve?*

If anyone says 'no', they keep going. If everyone says 'yes', the team leaves with a real decision—one that people are committed to.

> Consensus and agreement are not the same."
>
> **Key learnings:** Get everyone thinking for themselves, sharing their perspectives, having a voice. This will result in faster decision making.

Dedicate

Teams need to be aligned and committed to the way forward as a team. This means the team has a united front and voice outside of the team. The team is clear on what the decision is, and how it will be communicated beyond the team. Dedicate means there is a commitment to action. There are no side conversations, meetings after meetings, or saying, "We are doing this, but what I really think is that ..." We are ready to move to action and deliver. Dedication is where the accountability comes in.

There's a big difference between *agreement* and *alignment*. You might not love the decision, but you back it. You give it a red-hot go. That's alignment. And it's what high-performing teams do.

This model suggests that once you dedicate and commit to a decision, it is final and done. In reality, we know that life isn't that linear; there are times we need to realign, pivot, and change decisions. Communicate and realign when this occurs, so everyone is on the same page.

Dedicate is team alignment. We will explore this more in Chapter 12 – Team Alignment.

Thriving teams have healthy debate. They diagnose the key challenge, have generative dialogue, decide together, and dedicate to decisions that are made.

CHAPTER 11

Learning

Thriving teams are learning teams,
and so that means leaning into curiosity.

— Amy Edmondson, on the *Thriving Leaders Podcast*

Teams learn just as individuals do. They learn from their successes, mistakes, and failures. It is important to create this reflective practice as a team, so they learn, grow, adapt, and evolve. Individuals and the team develop in parallel. Team learning requires psychological safety as people need to be vulnerable and not fear taking risks.

We need to set the stage for learning as a team. Make this learning culture expectation explicit. Build in mechanisms for teams to learn, and integrate this into their work. I hear from teams that they don't have time for learning, or there is so much change that they can't keep up. This is why it needs to be built into how teams work. A lot of learning will happen on the job or through peer coaching and mentoring, rather than through formal training.

In our conversation on the *Thriving Leaders Podcast*, Amy Edmondson explained what true psychological safety looks like: "Psychological safety is a learning environment. It's a climate where people believe they can take the interpersonal risks that learning requires. Things like asking for help, pointing out a mistake, sharing a crazy idea, or experimenting—these are all learning behaviours. But they don't have guaranteed results. And as human beings, we tend to prefer certainty."

A recent study (*Harvard Business Review*, 2025), looked at over 160 innovation teams and found the importance of understanding your team's learning rhythm. It is not only about how much the team learns, but also when and how they learn. Here are four ways teams learn:

- **Reflexive:** Assessing strategies, revisiting goals, and discussing challenges.
- **Experiential:** Brainstorming, prototyping, and testing new ideas.
- **Contextual:** Scanning the environment for trends, signals, and shifts.
- **Vicarious:** Drawing lessons from others who've done similar work.

The study found that the most effective teams didn't feel they needed to do everything, but would bookend their learning with reflexive learning, to consolidate a shared understanding. They found that high-performing teams intentionally structure learning by building in time for reflection, distinguishing exploration from refinement, and ingraining predictable learning cycles.

A learning culture within a team balances psychological safety and accountability. Ways to create a learning culture within a team include:

- Celebrate success.
- Learn from mistakes and failures.
- Encourage experimentation and risk-taking.

- Create a culture of feedback.
- Develop new skills.
- Create a team learning plan.

🌐 REAL-WORLD CASE STUDY

Using data to lift team performance

The AOC didn't just survive the Tokyo Games—they learned from them. Speaking on the *Thriving Leaders Podcast*, Matt Carroll shared that after the Tokyo Games, hard data showed illness rates were almost zero—and that the athletes who competed in the second week were fitter and better supported than ever before. Why? Because under COVID protocols, everyone had to leave the Olympic Village within 48 hours of finishing their events. That meant less illness, more focused resources, and a stronger second-week performance overall.

Matt said: *"We took that learning and applied it to Paris. We introduced a new rule: athletes must leave the village within 48 hours of finishing competition—not because of a health order, but because it actually worked. It's about protecting the high-performance environment for the entire team.*

There was resistance at first, naturally. People want to celebrate. But once athletes talked among themselves—swimmers speaking to runners, for example—they started to see the benefit."

It's a great example of how you build on experience, use data to back your decisions, and set a higher standard for the next cycle.

Celebrate success

Teams often don't pause to reflect on what they have achieved. Make success visible. Build this into your meeting rhythms and ensure this is shared beyond the team. Publicly acknowledge and celebrate achievements to reinforce the positive impact of learning. When we succeed, we can still learn and improve further. Acknowledge examples of teamwork when team members work cohesively together. This positive reinforcement will encourage other team members to do the same.

Share team successes and reflect:

- How can we do more of this?
- What did we learn from this?
- How can we leverage this strength next time?
- What could we do differently next time?

Teams, like individuals, need fresh and exciting challenges to stay motivated. These present learning opportunities for the team—utilising the skills they have today, and the future skills they have the potential to develop.

The Managing Director of my international insurance client has disrupted his long-tenured team by moving leaders into different roles outside their areas of expertise. For example, from Risk to People & Culture. These lateral moves helps team members continue to learn and stay motivated and gives them a breadth of experience. This also demonstrates to the team that their skills and potential are valued— another way to celebrate their success.

Learn from mistakes and failures

When I interviewed Amy Edmonson for my *Thriving Leaders Podcast*, it was a big deal for me. You can hear it at the end, when I embarrassingly gush over meeting my work hero. What I haven't shared with many people is what happened afterwards. I was on cloud nine—more elated and prouder than I'd felt writing my first book. And then, in the space of minutes, I went from the highest high to the lowest low.

This was the first time I'd used Squadcast, a podcasting platform. I'd done a practice run with Jo, our Learning & Marketing Designer in our team at Thriving Culture, knowing it was new to me and that this session was incredibly important. After the interview, I went to upload the recording. It took ages ... and when it finished, I discovered I only had my video and audio—Amy's were missing.

I tried to stay calm and got on to tech support (aka my husband, Ben). For the next half hour, Jo, Ben, and I searched everywhere to try to find where the file had been saved. But it was gone. My heart sank. I'd just wasted an hour of Amy Edmondson's time!

Rushing through my mind was Amy's insights on failure. My mistake was a *basic failure*—one that absolutely could've been prevented. Thankfully, Jo eventually found the file. It had been saved in some obscure folder. The crisis was over, it was now downgraded to a mistake.

When we fail, our heart races. We go into fight-or-flight mode. And we don't operate at our best. What I learned was simple: ask podcast guests to leave their browser window open for 5–10 minutes after we finish recording to make sure the upload completes. Since then, I've never had the same issue. We all learn from failure. This one was a near miss—but the lesson stuck.

💡 **THOUGHT LEADER INSIGHTS**

Amy Edmondson on mistakes, failure, and intelligent risk

On the *Thriving Leaders Podcast*, Amy Edmonson explained that there's a critical difference between mistakes and failures—and many languages don't even have separate words for them.

She offered the following definitions:

- Mistake—an unintended deviation from a known practice or process. We all make them, but the goal is to minimise the ones that really matter, especially when the stakes are high.
- Failure—an undesired outcome. Some failures are devastating (like a plane crash), others are just part of learning, like a failed lab experiment that brings valuable insight.

She identified three types of failures:

1. Basic failures—caused by mistakes, are preventable.
2. Complex failures—multiple things go wrong at once.
3. Intelligent failures—the kind we should welcome, especially when experimenting in new territory.

Amy recommends that we should prevent failure in familiar territory, both basic and complex. Then, create environments of risk-taking where we can engage in smart experiments and value intelligent failure.

As she explained:

"The best organisations—especially those that rely on innovation—send a clear message: If you're not failing, you're not doing your job.

Safe, predictable success means you're only doing what's already known. Real growth comes from trying new things, even if they don't work. That's a framing move—making sure people are on the same page about what sport we're playing."

Key learnings: A thriving team will sometimes end in success, and sometimes in intelligent failure. Either way, welcome the new information, learn from it, and value it.

Learning is uncomfortable. The fear of getting it wrong can impede intelligent failures. We need to normalise mistakes and failures as an opportunity to learn and grow. When we ask lots of questions, it shows that we don't have the answers and we are all learning. Equally important is to discuss failures openly and constructively, extracting lessons and applying them in future endeavours.

When things don't go to plan, see it as an opportunity to learn what is really happening. Teams should regularly report bad news. Teams that hide bad news and only report the positives lack psychological safety. Blameless reporting helps organisations learn. Speak up when there is an ambiguous threat, as you may be risking a major failure for not speaking up due to not knowing for certain (Edmondson, 2019, 2023).

Failure can feel unpleasant, but it is part of life, and our attitudes towards it and as a team influence how we learn. When teams or individuals are consistently failing or making mistakes there could be a performance issue.

Encourage experimentation and risk-taking

Innovative companies like Atlassian and Google are known for their experimentation culture. The level of risk-taking and experimentation should fit your organisation's culture. Experiment as a team in the service of learning.

Agile teams have built a culture that emphasises failing fast. They have built in learning loops, rather than waiting until the end of the project delivery. This helps teams stay on track, innovate, and learn. Agile teams naturally have a learning culture. They have built in a mindset of failing fast, and they have retrospective meetings to learn. It's built into their operating rhythm.

Encourage learning by setting up small experiments and trying new approaches in bite-sized ways. Make it clear that you want your team to share ideas—no matter how 'out there' they might be—without worrying about judgement. If something doesn't go to plan, avoid the blame game. Instead, treat it as a chance to reflect, adapt, and come back stronger. By taking calculated risks yourself, you're showing that this isn't just lip service—you genuinely support experimentation and continuous improvement.

Just as importantly, build in regular check-ins so there's always space to talk through wins and failures. Teams can get busy and rush on to the next project, forgetting to celebrate successes or review failures for insights. Feedback loops are important, so people see that every outcome—good or bad—moves the whole group forward.

Ask yourself, what's one experiment we are running this quarter?

Ensure you praise staff for taking initiative, even if this means failure. This instils self-belief and confidence, and creates a culture of taking risks and innovation. Encourage an experimentation mindset.

Create a culture of feedback

Professor of Psychology at Stanford University, Carol Dweck, coined the term 'growth mindset' to describe the way people think about ability, intelligence, and talent. A growth mindset is the belief that feedback and failure are chances to learn and grow, and that you can improve over time. A fixed mindset is the belief that your abilities are innate and set—you see feedback and failure as a personal attack. Learning requires us to adopt a growth mindset and approach it with curiosity. We want to encourage a team growth mindset.

Teams should normalise feedback. It should come from peers as well as the leader. Sharing thoughts on progress, offering advice, and providing support are essential. Put systems or ways of working in place that build feedback loops into your rhythm. Role model not just giving feedback—but also receiving it.

This creates opportunities to help team members work through challenges and roadblocks. When we avoid conversations or delay feedback, we're not creating a culture of learning—we're creating a culture of fear. Feedback doesn't need to be punitive; it's an opportunity for the team to learn and grow.

One Team feedback

Sometimes team feedback shows up in hidden cues, like leading or repeated questions. That's often a sign it's time for a more direct, feedback-rich conversation.

Talk as a team about what gets in the way of giving feedback. Common barriers include fear of damaging relationships, people's reactions, and poor timing. Encourage the team to reframe feedback as a shared opportunity to learn and grow.

Get the team to practise giving feedback to each other. One exercise I use (which usually feels uncomfortable or confronting at first) is called One Team feedback. First, I teach the team how to give actionable feedback—and how to receive it. Then we create a psychologically safe environment for giving peer-to-peer feedback as a group. This can be done as a whole team or in a short, one-on-ones. I give people time to prepare their feedback using two prompts:

- The single most important contribution their teammate makes to the team.
- One area they could improve for the greater good of the team.

After everyone has delivered their feedback, each person shares what they heard or took away. They walk away having received both positive and constructive feedback from the entire team.

There are always a few people who feel apprehensive at the start. But by the end of the session, people feel energised—like a weight has been lifted. I recommend doing this twice a year. It's a great way to build the feedback muscle and face into difficult conversations together. It also strengthens relationships. (Important note: I wouldn't recommend this if psychological safety is low.)

Make it a habit to give positive feedback to your teammates. Go beyond "good job" or "thanks"—be specific. Targeted positive feedback not only helps individuals learn and grow, but also lifts the whole team. Positive reinforcement is a powerful motivator.

Regular individual and team reflections

Build in feedback mechanisms as a team. That could include retrospectives, after-action reviews, or post-implementation reviews. Reflection and feedback loops are vital.

It's important the team takes time to reflect on how it's operating. This could be a quarterly check-in to assess whether you're living your purpose and values, and whether you're demonstrating the behaviours you agreed on.

Create space for honest, generative dialogue. Ask:

- What's working well?
- What can be improved?
- How vulnerable has the team been lately—on a scale of 1–10?

Develop new skills

Teams need to adapt to change and complexity. Technologies, geopolitical tensions, markets changing, and stakeholder and client expectations evolve. This requires teams to evolve also.

This matters more than ever. As leadership expert and author Jennifer Garvey Berger says, teams need to build 'complexity fitness'—the ability to hold multiple perspectives, navigate tensions, and work with ambiguity, not against it. That's a muscle we need to strengthen together. When a team practises curiosity, challenges assumptions, and learns in real time, they become more resilient, adaptable, and united.

💡 THOUGHT LEADER INSIGHTS

Create a team learning plan

David Clutterbuck recommends that teams create a team learning plan. On the *Thriving Leaders Podcast*, he described it as the link between the business plan and an individual learning plan—a quarterly rhythm where the team asks:

- What learning do we need as a team and as individuals?
- How will we support each other?
- Who's responsible for what kind of learning?

He said, *"It's a constantly rolling plan, and the team regularly asks themselves:*

- *Are we evolving fast enough?*
- *Do we have the capabilities we'll need in the next 12 months?*
- *Do we need a team coach?*
- *What training do we need to invest in?*
- *What AI capability do we need within the team?"*

David said answering these questions might mean learning to contribute more effectively in meetings, or picking up new technology skills.

Key learnings: Teams learn just as individuals learn. Create a plan so you can be intentional about the collective learning the team needs to undertake.

Support

Thriving teams support each other. They have each other's backs. Using collaborative language like *we* and *us* signals that the team is in it together. The words we use matter.

Support can come in all shapes and sizes. Thriving teams need to know they can count on their teammates to follow through on commitments. When there are trusting relationships in place, team members feel comfortable sharing if they're struggling to meet a deadline or if they lack the capability and need someone else's skills. That kind of honesty only happens when people feel safe enough to speak up—and when they know they won't be judged for it.

Being able to rely on one another for support builds strength. It's not a weakness to ask for help—it's a sign of a strong team. Peer and team building expert Leo Bottary explained on the *Thriving Leaders Podcast,* you can't be afraid to ask for help. In many workplaces, people see asking for help as a weakness—it makes them feel incompetent or helpless. But successful people see it differently. They view asking for help as an act of resourcefulness. They know they don't have all the answers and actively use the support and knowledge around them. Sometimes, it's also about *how* we ask. Saying "I need your help" can sound like a burden. But saying "I'd love your help on this" invites collaboration and acknowledges the other person's value. It shifts the tone from dependence to partnership.

With a bit of reframing, teams can start to see asking for help not as a flaw—but as a strength.

How do your team members challenge and support each other?

Engage in the learning process with your team and learn with them.

Challenge and Support

Challenge and support is critical for a thriving team. You are required to strike a balance between accountability and psychological safety. This means teams can have healthy, challenging debates.

Build this muscle with your team so that they can diagnose the problem to solve, have robust dialogue anchored in listening, asking, and sharing. Be clear as a team on how you will decide and ensure that everyone is on the same page. Teams need to dedicate themselves to decisions that are made. Be a united front as a team, which demonstrates their commitment and alignment.

Teams learn just as individuals do. They support each other. Adaptation requires us to learn, grow, and evolve together. Understand your team's learning rhythm. Build in opportunities for the team to reflect on their successes, failures, and mistakes. Be intentional in creating safe spaces for experimentation and risk-taking. See failure as an opportunity to learn and grow. Invest in your people to develop new skills. Build the feedback muscle in your team.

What thriving teams do differently:

- Have healthy challenging debate (diagnose, dialogue, decide, dedicate).
- They learn from their mistakes, failures, and successes.
- They support each other and have each other's backs.

Actions

1. **Introduce the healthy debate model to your team.** Explain the 4Ds and the elements to have a successful, healthy debate (diagnose, dialogue, decide, dedicate).

2. **Discuss as a team how you have healthy debate today.**
   - How do we decide the problem to solve?
   - How do we have a robust dialogue?
   - How do we make decisions as a team?
   - How do we commit to the decisions made?

   Based on the responses, identify the team's strengths and areas to improve.

3. **Facilitate your next team decision using this framework.** Have an observer who will provide feedback, say what you did well, and what you may need to try next time. Rotate this role in the future. This is helping the team learn.

4. **Determine the learning culture as a team.** Discuss as a team:
   - How do we celebrate success?
   - How do we learn from our mistakes and failures?
   - How do we experiment and take risks?
   - How do we provide feedback to each other?
   - How do we develop new skills?

5. **Create a team learning plan.** Based on the team's responses, craft a learning plan as a team.
   - What learning do we need as a team?
   - How will we support each other?

RESOURCES

www.thrivingculture.com.au/ttbook

PART 6

Alignment

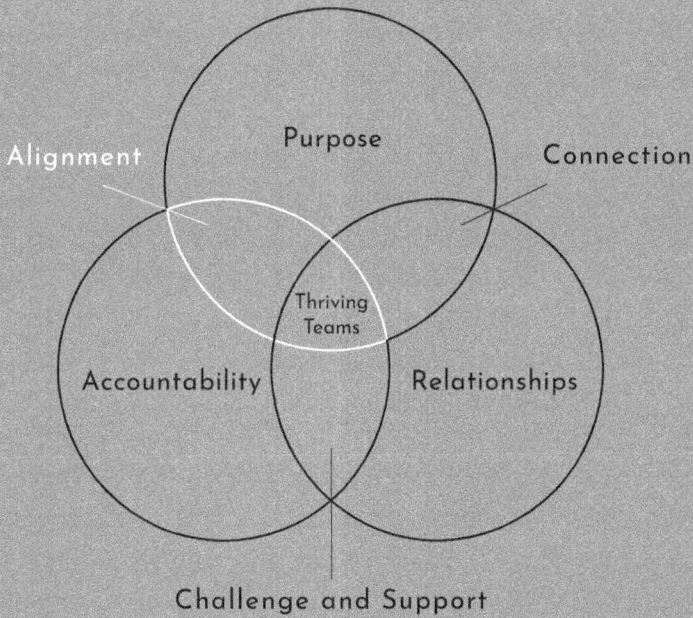

In a post-COVID world, are we less aligned and connected than ever before? We don't see our teams as frequently with hybrid work, which limits the number of corridor conversations. Anchor days encourage us to connect with our teams, but we don't always make intentional agreements to collaborate and engage face to face with stakeholders, which is driving further disconnect. The economic climate has been challenging, which has driven executives to focus on executing their strategy to ensure long-term viability. This has meant that we need, now more than ever, alignment and connection across teams to enable strategy.

According to Deloitte's 2025 *Human Capital Trends Report,* 41% of employees spend time on work that doesn't contribute to value creation. This lack of alignment means that we waste time on the wrong things, feel busy, and get overwhelmed. We end up in a cycle of doing lots of stuff, but potentially not focusing on the right things. This leads to stress, burnout, and presents a psychosocial risk within organisations.

Alignment is the final piece in the Thriving Teams Model. When we are aligned as a team we are all on the same page. We are a united front. In the Thriving Teams Model, Alignment sits between Purpose and Accountability. There is congruence between the two.

Teams need to be aligned and committed to the way forward. We also need alignment with stakeholders, who often will have conflicting priorities and expectations of us. Nurturing these relationships consistently is key.

We will discuss team alignment and stakeholder alignment in this part of the book.

CHAPTER 12

Team Alignment

If you want to go fast, go alone.
If you want to go far, go together.
— African Proverb

Alignment starts with the team. Team alignment is a shared understanding of the team's purpose, strategy, goals, and roles.

McKinsey 2024 Team Effectiveness study identified alignment as one of four critical drivers of team effectiveness. Research in neuroscience shows that collaborative work, where trust and aligned goals are present, stimulate oxytocin in the brain. This feel-good hormone enhances team problem-solving, resulting in improvement in the performance of complex tasks. Dopamine, our reward centre in the brain, increases when we make progress towards shared goals, reinforcing team collaboration and celebrating collective wins (Thompson, 2025; Zak, 2017).

Aligned teams prioritise team goals over individual goals. Your values and behaviours are congruent between individual and team goals, and between the team's purpose and the organisation's purpose. When team members help shape the team's direction, there's greater buy-in.

When alignment is strong, teams present a united front. Communication is consistent and clear. The team speaks with conviction about purpose, direction, and goals. Team alignment is a commitment to moving forward together. It's also at the heart of the 'dedicate' piece of the 4Ds of Healthy Debate. We just work better together when we are aligned.

You know your team is aligned when:

- There is a shared vision and a clear team purpose. (See Chapter 2 – Team Purpose)
- Everyone's clear on their role. (See Chapter 3 – Meaningful Work)
- Goals and strategy are well understood. (See Chapter 6 – Clear Direction)
- Accountability is shared. (See Chapter 7 – Team Accountability)
- People challenge and support each other. (See Part 5 – Challenge and Support)

🌐 REAL-WORLD CASE STUDY

Tokyo, teamwork, tuna and trust

Tokyo 2020 was held in the middle of a global pandemic. People were opposed to the Games going ahead. Empty stadiums, no crowds to cheer from the sidelines, border closures—it was like no other. Despite that, it was a success; not a single case of COVID in the Australian team. No breaches in the performance environment. It was also the first Olympics in which more female athletes participated than male athletes.

On the *Thriving Leaders Podcast* Matt Carroll joked: *"If it wasn't for the tuna fishermen of South Australia, we might never have made it to Tokyo. Japan Airlines had stopped carrying passengers, but they were still flying tuna. And that kept just enough aircraft in the sky for us to use."*

They worked across two teams, the 'home team' and the 'away team', especially during the Tokyo Games. The away team supported the athletes in Japan, and the home team supported the returning athletes by navigating the chaos of international quarantine, the changing border closures, and media narratives.

"At one point, we had more athletes in quarantine back home than we had competing in Japan. But both teams had to be completely aligned—one couldn't succeed without the other.

The key to making that work was trust. You've got to trust that your colleague has your back. That their work is just as important as yours. You can't have one part of the team saying, 'We're doing the real work', and the other feeling like they don't count. That's how things fall apart under pressure.

We built that trust by being crystal clear—what are we here to do? Who's going to do it? And how are we going to do it? And as leaders, we had to model it. People don't follow what you say—they follow what you do."

The whole team needed to be aligned and committed to what was to be achieved and how they were going to do it.

When teams aren't aligned, you'll hear or see:

- The meeting after the meeting.
- "Stay in your lane."
- "That's not my job."
- A gap between what's said and what's done.
- Comments that contradict the agreed direction.
- Goals that sound good but lack meaning.
- Ambiguity or role creep.
- Fragmented or siloed work.
- Constantly conflicting priorities.

When you notice misalignment within the team, it needs to be shared. Use language such as "I've noticed" or "I've observed" when delivering the feedback. Offer this as an observation and see what others have observed and what their interpretation of this is. As a team, discuss how you can address the misalignment.

Shared goals need clear roles

When teams have shared goals or are delivering on strategy, we need clarity on who's doing what. Job descriptions help, but they're rarely enough. We need to know who's accountable and who's contributing—and ensure the work is evenly distributed.

The RACI model is a useful tool to clarify this:

- **Responsible:** The person (or people) doing the work.
- **Accountable:** The single person with ultimate ownership and decision-making authority.
- **Consulted:** People whose input, advice, or expertise you need.
- **Informed:** People who need to be kept up to date on progress and decisions.

It's a great way to map deliverables and ensure everyone's clear on their role—and just as importantly, who the stakeholders are. It also ensures your team is aligned on priorities and avoids stepping on each other's toes.

Realignment

Roles and responsibilities may need a reset as things change. It's about regularly getting on the same page around goals, priorities, and expectations.

Realignment might mean checking the team hasn't drifted off course—especially if the goalposts have shifted or external factors have brought in new challenges.

You might need to revisit your team's principles (meetings, communication, prioritisation), or reflect on whether your purpose and values still hold true.

Sometimes, it's also about navigating conflicting priorities—getting clear on what matters most, making hard choices, and getting the balance right between BAU and strategic priorities.

Collaboration

When we collaborate, we work together towards shared goals. It's about building strong relationships based on trust, psychological safety, open communication, and diverse perspectives. Collaboration means sharing information, challenging ideas, and getting creative. That's where innovation and great business outcomes come from.

True collaboration puts the work between us—it's not about individual brilliance, but shared ownership. The 'dialogue' piece of the 4Ds of Healthy Debate reminds us to listen to learn, ask curious questions, and share perspectives and knowledge. This is at the heart of strong collaboration.

Be intentional with who and how you collaborate. What are the conversations that are needed to occur? Put more attention and intention into the collaboration, so you are more courageous. This helps build relationships with your peers.

Collaboration needs to extend beyond your team.

CHAPTER 13

Stakeholder Alignment

Individually, we are one drop.
Together, we are an ocean.

— Ryunosuke Satoro

Teams don't work in isolation; they are part of a complex system. For an organisation to be high performing, it requires teams working together to deliver outcomes. This requires horizontal leadership, breaking down silos, and building strong stakeholder relationships.

Social capital refers to the value created through relationships and networks between individuals, groups, and communities. This intangible asset helps people collaborate, share knowledge and information, and innovate. There are three main elements of social capital:

- **Bonds:** Close-knit relationships, like family, close friends and homogeneous teams. Great for social support, but can limit innovation and creativity.
- **Bridges:** Weaker connections, such as acquaintances or cross-functional teams. These bridges are important for sharing information and resources and delivering on strategy.

- **Links:** Connections that go beyond hierarchy or organisational boundaries. These are key influences, authority, and people who hold power. These links unlock access to resources beyond your network.

Thriving teams need a mixture of networks. They build strong, trusting bonds within their team, they build bridges and connections to other teams, and they link upwards and outwards by building relationships with authority and influencers. When considering stakeholder alignment, we must consider the networks we hold and their effectiveness.

Don't fall into the trap of only building networks with people who are like us. Diversity in networks is essential. Be clear about the relevant relationships and their purpose, especially the bridging and linking relationships.

Stakeholders can be other teams within your organisation, partner organisations, vendors, regulators, industry bodies, the board, community groups, customers, or clients, to name a few. These are all crucial stakeholders that the team needs to engage with to be successful. Developing, building, and maintaining these relationships is critical for the success of the team.

Stakeholder relationships

We need each other. People get the work done. Don't be insular and operate in a vacuum as a team. Lift your gaze and be strategic with the relationships that you need to build, nurture, or repair.

Think about the networks and webs that are most important for your team to be successful within the organisation. How can you bridge these invisible gaps that exist to improve alignment, understanding, relationships, and connection? It is the gaps that trip up teams.

This is about human connection. The 'dialogue' part of 4Ds is essentially a collaboration model. Use the core skills when collaborating with stakeholders; listen to learn, ask curious questions, and share your perspective.

Sometimes we don't engage at all, simply because we forget. Other times, we avoid it as it feels too hard. Or we engage too late. Engage early, if you can, to avoid misalignment. The stakeholders will have more buy-in to the solution as they will feel part of developing it.

How does it feel when you get a call only when something has gone wrong? On the flip side, early engagement means you are bringing the team in. Proactive engagement builds relationships, buy-in, and also puts accountability back on them. When we are always reactive, we feel like we are firefighting, we start on the back foot, and relationships get strained. This makes work that needs to be done in the future harder.

Create networks of connected people and teams to learn together, adapt, and experiment.

Look at your stakeholders as key partners to your team's success.

🌐 REAL-WORLD CASE STUDY

Stakeholder alignment is a two-way street

Australian athletes give their best, and the AOC must ensure they are supported with the best opportunity for success. As a member-based organisation—from tennis through to curling—the AOC doesn't just deliver for itself, but for the sports it represents. Aligning stakeholders is therefore essential to fulfilling its charter and organisational purpose.

As Matt Carroll said in the *Thriving Leaders Podcast*: *"The athletes we take to the Games don't belong to us. We borrow them from our member sports, and that means the sports have to trust us too. That trust has to be earned. We created a series of CEO roundtables—three a year—just to talk, to listen, and to work out how we could do things better, together. It's the same with the government, commercial partners, and sponsors. You can't assume they know what you do. A government minister once said to me, 'Matt, never presume we know—and never presume our advisers do either.' That stuck with me. So, we built materials to explain exactly what we do and how we fit into the broader system.*

Even with sponsors, we'd ask: What do you want out of this partnership? Because if it doesn't work for them, they won't stick around. Alignment only works when it's a two-way street."

Building strong stakeholder relationships has been key to the AOC's success.

Stakeholder mapping

To effectively manage and engage stakeholders, teams need to step back and identify, assess, and plan how to engage with them. This isn't about stripping away the natural, organic way relationships form. It's about being thoughtful—who are our most critical stakeholders? And being intentional—who in the team should engage them and how?

Start by identifying your key stakeholders. Then do a stakeholder mapping exercise.

This could be as simple as mind-mapping on a whiteboard with your team, the most critical relationships for your team.

Use red, orange, and green markers:

- **Red:** The relationship is weak or strained.

- **Orange:** There's room to improve.
- **Green:** The relationship is strong and productive.

Decide who in your team will manage each relationship.

If you need more detail—especially for teams managing a large number of relationships—create a Stakeholder Matrix. I like to overlay this with Mendelow's Power–Interest Grid.

Power (influence) refers to the ability to impact outcomes, decisions, and directions.

Interest refers to how much they care or are involved.

Based on their level of power/influence, and interest, determines how you manage them.

- High Power/Influence and High Interest: Manage closely (key player, engage actively and often).
- High Power/Influence and Low Interest: Keep satisfied (involve when necessary, keep information relevant and sharp).
- Low Power/Influence and High Interest: Keep Informed (maintain communication so they understand decisions and leverage their enthusiasm).
- Low Power/Influence and Low Interest: Monitor (Minimal engagement, check in occasionally in case things change).

What to include in a stakeholder matrix:

- Stakeholder name.
- Interest level (high/low).
- Influence level (high/low).
- Stakeholder's need (manage closely, keep satisfied, keep informed, monitor).
- Faction or beliefs (what they stand for or care about).
- Engagement strategy.

- Who is accountable for the relationship (refer to RACI for definition).
- Who is responsible for the relationship (refer to RACI for definition).
- Last engaged/notes.

Revisit this quarterly as a team. This shouldn't turn into admin overload—it's a conversation tool, not a reporting exercise. The goal is to stay intentional about your relationships so you're engaging the right people at the right time to ensure your team's success.

Identify your advocates and sponsors. Know who is in your corner. You won't win over everyone, but make sure you can name your advocates and your sponsors. Advocates back your work because they believe in what you're doing. Sponsors hold power. They'll go into bat for you when it counts. You need both—so keep them close.

Notice roles and patterns within the system. Discuss these with the team and with your stakeholders where appropriate.

Factions and politics

Politics exist within every organisation. The extent differs. Whether it's how strategic decisions are made, turf wars over resources and projects, or other power plays, acting politically is required of leaders and shouldn't necessarily be viewed as a bad thing. It is about how you influence and use your authority to shape outcomes that matters.

Stakeholders are groups of people with whom you need to engage. Factions are groups that share common beliefs, values, and loyalties. These are especially important when navigating adaptive challenges. Those that are messy, complex, and don't have a clear solution. People may assume you hold certain beliefs based on your characteristics, such as your gender, role, or team affiliation. But belonging to a stakeholder group doesn't necessarily mean you share their perspective. This is why understanding factions matters. They cut across role titles, teams, and stakeholder groups. Factions represent people's loyalties, fears, and what they're willing to defend or lose. We need to stop assuming and start asking and listening.

Factions form around perspectives—where people sit in the organisation, their role, and their values. Understanding why they're showing up, what they care about, and how it connects to the purpose—that's where alignment begins. Teams need to stay together and work through challenges, even when it's uncomfortable

Leaders must create holding environments, spaces where people can explore the mess, name the real issue, and take shared ownership.

💡 THOUGHT LEADER INSIGHTS

Naming factions

Kaye Monk-Morgan is the President and CEO of the Kansas Leadership Centre, which develops excellence in civic leadership development and engagement. She works with communities and organisations across the United States on some of the messiest challenges leaders face.

On the *Thriving Leaders Podcast*, Kaye shared about how to lead when stakes are high. She recommends to start with a collective purpose, then be explicit about the factions (the different reasons people show up) and build trustworthy, transparent processes so people can disagree safely and still move forward together.

"It is about collective purpose. Being intentional about sharing what the work is, and why we do the work. Whether it's internal or external groups, folks show up to a cause with a different purpose. I may care about homelessness as a citizen, someone else cares as a person who was previously unhoused,

> *and someone as an elected official. You need to own the positionality and why you show up for that faction.*
>
> *Overlay the stakeholders and the factions to alleviate some of the discomfort by being really clear. If you ask, then people are really excited to share. I think it is one of the most genuine ways to invite people into partnership.*
>
> *We talk about being vulnerable, creating systems where we're speaking truth. If we trust the process, then I don't have to trust you. If we build a process that is transparent enough that I can trust you, and I hear you from your heart to my heart, that makes it a little bit easier in our team to make progress."*
>
> **Key learnings:** In every adaptive challenge, there are factions. We don't always name them and when we don't name them, they harden into silos, politics, and resistance.

We often operate on the assumption of what others' views, beliefs, or loyalties might be, rather than gathering the voices in the room. If you ask people, they are often excited about sharing their point of view.

Acting politically is not a bad thing. It means you understand how the system works, how to build coalitions, where the barriers are, and how to navigate them. It's when it's done without integrity that it becomes icky. Being politically savvy is necessary if you're going to lead.

When we are dealing with competing loyalties and factions, work avoidance is common.

Authority and influence

People have different reactions to authority figures. There is formal authority based on your role and informal authority based on your influence. Everybody can exercise leadership, no matter what your role in the organisation is. When we think about stakeholders, we can use our authority (power) or influence. Understand what authority and influence you have with stakeholders. Be strategic with how you use this. Leverage different authority and influence within the team with stakeholders. Based on relationships or role titles, certain team members may be better placed to influence stakeholders.

Challenging authority can be risky, so make sure you challenge the idea, the status quo, or system—not the person.

THOUGHT LEADER INSIGHTS

Authority and influence in decision-making

On the *Thriving Leaders Podcast*, Kaye Monk-Morgan shared that you may have authority, but that doesn't mean people are going to follow you. You earn that through relationships, through listening, and through showing that you understand the work. Authority is the right to make decisions, but it doesn't mean you have influence.

"Leadership is mobilising people to make progress on really tough issues. Anyone can lead, anytime and anywhere. It's not reserved for people with title and position.

It's a place for strong authority. For authority to be much more engaged in protection, direction, and order. In our lexicon, our invitation for everyone to exercise leadership does not mean everybody gets to be the boss. It does mean that everyone can see and seize a moment to engage around an issue that they care about, from their point of view, and can help move that forward.

There are days I want to come in and say, 'Just do it because I said so'. But that usually doesn't work. Instead I ask myself 'What's a question I can ask?'"

Kaye and her team embrace accountability. For her, leadership means owning both actions and outcomes—while giving people the space to exercise autonomy and agency.

"We try to differentiate between who the decision-making authorities are, who is accountable for the outcome, and who is responsible for implementation."

Key learnings: The most impactful people in organisations are often the ones without titles—but they hold trust, credibility, and influence. That's real power.

Cross-functional collaboration

Cross-functional collaboration requires people, teams, and networks of people across the organisation to work together. It can be challenging when there are silos, we are reactive, and power dynamics are at play. We often default to authority to solve our problems, and worse yet, if there is unhealthy politics at that level, it is even harder to get the work done.

THOUGHT LEADER INSIGHTS

Informal networks that get the work done

David Clutterbuck's 'teams of teams' work explores what he call 'streams of connectedness'. These are the informal networks that form between teams—the sort of hidden substrate of the organisation.

According to David, leadership is made up of three functions:

1. Spotting something that needs attention.
2. Figuring out how to deal with it.
3. Making sure it gets done.

Those three things often don't sit with one person—they're distributed across people in informal systems. And many of these people don't appear anywhere in the official talent pool data. They're exercising leadership through influence, not authority.

He estimates that around 40% of critical decision-making in organisations happens through informal systems. It's very much a finger-in-the-air statistic—but when you start looking for it, you see it everywhere.

He gave the following anecdote from the banking sector:

"A customer walks into a branch with a really unusual problem. The branch sorts it by going through someone in head office. It gets resolved, but it's treated as a one-off—an anomaly.

Now, imagine that this same 'anomaly' is showing up in 20 or 30 branches across the country. Still, no one connects the dots—because there's no network to link those experiences. But once you create informal groups that start to flag these outliers, you turn anomalies into trends. And when a trend is recognised, that's when someone takes responsibility for it.

We found that a huge amount of decision-making and responsibility-taking happens outside the formal hierarchy."

Key learnings: Understand the informal networks within the system. Look for patterns and trends in your organisation to understand how work is getting done.

We need to collaborate across organisational boundaries. Often, the way organisations are structured, how people are rewarded, and the culture inhibit our ability to do this. Even with matrixed models, which aim to break down these barriers, they can unintentionally create tensions. Heidi Gardner, author of *Smart Collaboration* and *Smarter Collaboration*, says that collaboration goes beyond working together; it is about integrating diverse expertise across boundaries to address complex, high-stakes problems. These boundaries could include functions, geography, generations, or organisations. This requires intentionally sourcing deep expertise and knowledge across diverse domains.

Cross-border collaboration comes with immense friction. Cultural differences, language barriers, time zone differences, and often matrix model reporting lines all add to the complexity. There is considerable autonomy when teams work across borders.

That said, collaboration can get out of hand. Gartner's research found that 78% of organisational leaders report experiencing collaboration drag: excessive meetings, consensus-seeking, too much time seeking buy-in from stakeholders, too much peer feedback, unclear decision-making authority, or unnecessary reporting (*Harvard Business Review*, 2024). Set boundaries to prevent collaboration from becoming counterproductive.

Adam Kahane is a Canadian facilitator who has been involved in conflict resolution and systems change in South Africa, Colombia, and other complex civil society issues. In his book *Collaborating with the Enemy*, he explains that we don't always need to collaborate, it is a choice. We can choose to:

- **Collaborate:** Try to move forward together, even when you don't agree or aren't aligned on everything.
- **Force:** Try to change or stop them, but know it can escalate conflict and destroy trust.
- **Adapt:** Adjust to their position to stay in the game. Use when the stakes are high, aren't worth a fight, or you're trying to preserve harmony.
- **Exit:** When change is impossible and the cost of staying is too high.

When deciding what option is best, you need to weigh up the opportunities and risks of each option. This framework is extremely useful when dealing not only with internal stakeholders, but external stakeholders to the organisation.

Getting aligned

Misalignment is often a symptom of deeper, systemic issues. Common areas of misalignment are competing priorities; communication breakdowns; unclear roles, responsibilities, and accountability; and cultural ways of working.

Each team has their own priorities and expectations for their teams, and potentially yours too. What we deem as most important may be different from our stakeholders. Also, we have multiple stakeholders with different needs and expectations, which creates more complexity.

There are always trade-offs. Balancing competing priorities while navigating a political landscape is part of the game. To work through this, teams need to take a systemic approach to problem-solving—one that bridges the gaps between individuals, teams, and stakeholder groups.

Teaching people to zoom out and see the bigger system they're working within is essential. Without it, we default to blame and finger-pointing.

It's human nature to think that we individually are doing our bit, and that the people around us aren't. I see this play out in employee engagement data with clients, time and time again. The 'I' questions or 'my team' questions come back as the highest scoring results. But the 'my organisation' or 'senior leaders' or 'other teams' questions are almost always lower. When I hear "Our team is doing our bit. Stakeholders aren't", it tells me that people don't see the shared system they are in. (This links closely to collective accountability in Chapter 7 – Team Accountability.)

So, how do we deal with conflicting priorities? Every individual has their own priorities. So do teams. So do stakeholders. Perfect alignment across all three? That's utopia. It's rare.

In a high-stakes, complex environment, achieving alignment with teams and stakeholders requires working with people we disagree with or distrust. In *Collaborating with the Enemy*, Adam Kahane introduces stretch collaboration which embraces conflict, experimentation, and rapid feedback loops. It requires you to let go of the illusion of control, be open and flexible, and be willing to change your contribution, behaviours and assumptions, and how you are participating. This focus on self-change rather than trying to change others sees tangible progress.

When you are misaligned, priorities shift, or things get tense, try this:

1. **Start with curiosity and not assumptions.**
   - **Get on the same page:** Have a conversation about what matters most right now and the shared challenge.
   - **Put the work between you:** Step out of positional thinking and get curious about the challenge you're both facing.
   - **Understand their needs by asking questions:** Don't assume you know what's important to them. Stakeholders come with different agendas, and that's not a bad thing—it's just reality. Your job is to surface them.
   - **Share your priorities and capacity:** Let them understand what's important to you, your team, and why.

2. **Face into the tension.**
   - **Find the points of intersection:** What do you both care about? Where is the common ground? What are your shared goals?
   - **Don't ignore the points of difference:** Task conflict leads to innovation. It is a productive part of the process and not something we should ignore, even if it feels uncomfortable.
   - **Be open and flexible:** All strong relationships require compromise and a balance of needs. This isn't about giving in—it's about getting aligned enough to move forward. This means sharing your needs and being open to understanding theirs.
   - **Have a growth mindset and a willingness to learn:** We learn so much from our stakeholders, and if we lean in with curiosity and a growth mindset, we will be more open to experimentation.

3. **Get clear on the partnership going forward.**
   - **See stakeholders as partners:** Not blockers or distractions.
   - **Be clear on roles, responsibilities, and accountabilities:** Don't leave this to chance. Be explicit about what role each party will play and who has ultimate decision-making authority.
   - **Use collective language:** Such as 'we' and 'our'; this demonstrates that you are in this together, in true partnership.
   - **Agree next steps:** Even if you haven't reached a resolution, it is about making progress. This could be small experiments. Agree on what will happen next.

Sometimes this requires us to get multiple stakeholders together. Try to tackle the challenge in the system, rather than just seeing it from their perspective. This way, you can co-create what the priorities and trade-offs are together.

Interconnectedness and interdependence

When I work with senior leadership teams, such as the Executive Team and their direct reports, I facilitate an accountability exercise. People share what they are accountable for and the impact it has. We repeat the exercise and when we debrief it demonstrates the following things:

- We achieve a lot together.
- Our work is more interdependent than we realise.
- We need each other to be successful.

Senior leadership teams are one of the most important groups of leaders within the organisation. Some view these forums as tokenistic, and depending on how they are facilitated, they can be. These groups of leaders operationalise strategy, deliver change, and communicate it to their people. The core reason I believe these leaders need to get together is to build relationships and capability, so they can do the work that is required outside of their forums. This is where the One Team mindset discussed in Chapter 1 comes to life, and silos are broken down.

This area seems to be a massive focus for organisations. The economic climate has been tough, so organisations have a laser focus on operationalising their strategy. This is not possible if teams don't work together to deliver outcomes.

Looking at how your senior leaders operate together is a great reflection of how the system is really working. All leaders play a role in influencing how their teams collaborate; however, the way in which senior leaders behave really trickles through the organisation.

Cross-functional collaboration needs to happen at every layer within the organisation. When teams jump into action without engaging the right people and teams, outcomes get impacted.

Horizontal leadership, rather than the typical top-down approach, helps leaders lift their gaze and collaborate more readily across boundaries. It focuses on peers, within teams, and across teams collaborating together.

Operationalising strategy

It's one thing to have a strategy—it's another to actually implement it.

Strategy requires collaboration. Teams need to work across boundaries, coordinate with each other, and deliver shared outcomes. Priorities often have interdependencies that require realignment, negotiation, and trade-offs. Strong stakeholder relationships make this easier. This might involve working groups or teaming—bringing together people who don't usually work together. You might need to pull in subject matter experts from across the business to deliver on outcomes.

Cross-functional collaboration is critical to executing strategy. When people and teams collaborate well, they build trust, communicate better, and get things done faster. People need clarity on the actions and who's accountable. Address tensions between cross-functional teams to strengthen alignment and focus on the collective.

Strategic execution isn't failing because of the strategy itself—it's failing because the system around it is broken.

Operationalising strategy = alignment
+ collaboration + accountability

Here are the three levers that matter:

1. **Alignment** = Clarity and shared ownership.
2. **Collaboration** = How we work across functions.
3. **Accountability** = Follow-through and commitment to outcomes.

Strategy often feels too high-level, and BAU too operational. We need to bridge the gap and connect in the middle. It's the paradox of holding both—strategy *and* delivery. There's a tension there. Both are important. So how do you prioritise without just piling more on?

Stakeholder tensions are often not problems to be fixed, as that assumes someone is right and someone is wrong. Most of the time it's not that binary. These aren't problems to solve, but polarities to manage (Johnson, 1996, 2020). Polarity management supposes that there are two truths that we need to hold. Some of the common tensions between stakeholders include:

- BAU vs Strategy.
- Short-term vs Long-term.
- Risk vs Innovation.
- Speed vs Inclusion.
- Centralised vs Decentralised.

These tensions exist on a continuum and are ongoing balances. The goal isn't to pick a side, but to make intentional trade-offs. If you over-index on one, you risk backlash from another.

This is important for senior leaders to realise that it is an 'and' not an 'or'.

Identify the trade-offs and discuss them as a team and with stakeholders. Trade-offs could include resource allocation, operational efficiency, deprioritising low-impact BAU, or delaying some strategic priorities.

Sometimes teams need to say no to things. We are in this cycle of adding more, and often that means we need to stop something else or deprioritise it.

Holding stakeholders accountable

This is one of the most challenging things to do, when you don't have positional authority. However, it is critical to the success of a thriving team.

Provide feedback, seek to understand. Recalibrate expectations together of what is possible. Be transparent about what the next steps are. Focus on ideas and interests rather than making it personal.

If you or your team hasn't been accountable, own up to it. Share what you have learnt and what you are going to do to move the accountability forward. There is no point deflecting, avoiding, or minimising what has happened. Take ownership and come up with a solution to address this. Involve the relevant stakeholders as appropriate. Too many times we try to sweep things under the rug. Having conversations early and honestly is best to maintain the relationship longer term.

Be clear about the stakeholder relationships that are most critical. Build relationships and connections with critical stakeholders. Build networks at all levels within the organisation.

Alignment

Teams need to be aligned and committed to a unified way forward. This requires teams to dedicate and make commitments to their collective decisions. Teams don't need to agree; they need to align. Ensure that your team is on the same page. Play back what has been agreed and be really clear how you are going to take decisions forward. There will be times when you need to realign. Things change. Encourage collaboration. The 4D of healthy debate model is critical to team and stakeholder alignment.

Get really clear about who your critical stakeholders are as a team. Decide how you will nurture, maintain, and rebuild these relationships as required. Get the team together to map out your key stakeholders, and build this into your rhythm. Ensure alignment with stakeholders. When there is misalignment, start with curiosity and not assumptions, face into the tension, and get clear on the partnership going forward.

To operationalise strategy, it requires teams working together cross-functionally. Teams need to get aligned, collaborate, and be accountable. This is how the ripple of collective accountability happens, when teams are all working together.

What thriving teams do differently:

- Openly discuss misalignment as a team and with stakeholders.
- Actively manage stakeholder expectations, priorities, and relationships.
- Have a One Team mindset.

Actions

1. **Ensure clear roles and responsibilities as a team.** Discuss who is accountable and responsible for key initiatives and projects in the team. Remove any ambiguity.

2. **Discuss team alignment.** Check in regularly on team alignment. Share the observation and see what others have observed. Ask the team what their interpretation is. As a team, discuss how you can address the misalignment.
    *   Do we have a shared vision and a clear team purpose?
    *   Is everyone clear on their role and responsibilities?
    *   Are team goals and/or strategy well understood?
    *   Are we clear on how to hold each other accountable to these goals?

3. **Map your stakeholders.** Identify your critical stakeholders and their power and influence. Create intentional strategies as a team, being clear about who is accountable for the relationship. Create a regular operating rhythm to do this. Use the authority and influence within your team to engage stakeholders.

4. **Address stakeholder misalignment.** Get the right people together to discuss the misalignment. Start with curiosity and not assumptions, face into the tension, and get clear on the partnership going forward.

5. **Collaborate cross-functionally to operationalise strategy.** Actively collaborate, align, and get clear on accountabilities across organisational boundaries. Get your teams involved in these discussions, as often they will be managing relationships.

RESOURCES

www.thrivingculture.com.au/ttbook

Where to from here?

A thriving team knows why they exist, how to work together, what to work on, and when outcomes need to be achieved. A thriving team has a clear team purpose, strong relationships, psychological safety and trust, and accountability. They will challenge and support each other and learn together. Thriving teams are aligned and connected within and beyond the team.

Congratulations, you have made it to the end of the book. Now this is where the work begins. If you made it this far, it goes to show how much you care. You have the motivation and passion to build a team that people want to be part of. It is one thing to read and research what it takes to make a thriving team, but now it is on you to put this into practice.

I wrote this book to give you, the leader of the team, some practical and tangible tools to understand what is happening within your team. It may feel a bit overwhelming about where to start. My recommendation is to keep things simple, start conversations, and work through this as a team based on what is most important.

Use the Thriving Teams Diagnostic so that you know where to start. Use the resources in this book, via the QR codes or visit **thrivingculture.com/ttbook**. Experiment and make building a thriving team part of how you work.

Don't be hard on yourself; we will slip, make mistakes, and lose focus. It's about how we recover from these things that makes the difference.

Sustaining a thriving team is the biggest challenge. The bar lifts. Keeping each element of the Thriving Teams Model in mind helps alleviate this.

If you need help, sing out. I love working with teams across diverse industries. With an impartial team coach guiding the process, you can be part of the team.

Here are some ways we can work together:

- *Thriving Teams Programs:* build accountable, aligned and high-performing teams.
- *Leadership Development and Coaching:* grow confident, capable leaders.
- *Keynotes and Conferences:* energise your people with evidence-based, actionable insights.

To learn more, visit **thrivingculture.com.au**.

I'd love to stay connected and hear your thoughts about the book.

@ **claire.gray@thrivingculture.com.au**
in **linkedin.com/in/leadership-coach-facilitator**
[O] **@thriving.culture**

Good luck. You've got this.

Claire

Afterword

How do teams go from survival to revival to thrival? Two things count: what they pay attention to and the conversations they have about these. So much of management theory focuses on the traits and characteristics of the leader—yet the evidence suggests that the characteristics of the team are more significant in delivering consistent high performance. Teamwork is a partnership between leaders and team members, where everyone takes responsibility and accountability for both their own performance, learning, and wellbeing; and the performance, learning, and wellbeing of their colleagues.

As a team coach, my role is to support teams in having the conversations they need to have, but which for one reason or another have not yet been had. The reason for this is not just reticence to approach difficult topics. It is also inability to see the team's systems clearly. Teams that are not thriving fail to see the interconnections between assumptions and narratives, work processes, and communications that enhance or undermine collaborative endeavours. These systems are both internal and external. For example, the narratives that stakeholders hold are also influential in equipping the team to do its job.

Thriving teams pay high attention to continuous learning. If they stop learning, they cease to thrive. Thriving teams attend to each other and to their stakeholders, listening and adapting to maintain agility while not losing sight of their shared purpose. They are fun to be in, because they have *fizz* (enjoyment and purpose from the work they do) and *buzz* (enjoyment from the social environment with work colleagues).

Sadly, many if not most teams are stuck somewhere between survival and revival. Yet all it needs is to come together to have open and honest conversations about how the team functions and what they can collectively do about it. Sometimes it needs a team coach; sometimes a team leader with the courage to be more vulnerable with their team.

Claire Gray's *Thriving Teams* provides insights into the kind of co-learning conversations teams can have that help them break out of the rut and create an environment where the team thrives, along with everyone in it.

She translates decades of research into practical tools teams can use immediately—from clarifying shared purpose to embedding the ripple of accountability. In a world of teams of teams, everything is connected, and thriving is possible only when responsibility is distributed and shared across individuals, colleagues, and the wider system. These frameworks help leaders see their teams not as static groups, but as evolving systems with the capacity to adapt, align, and grow.

As you close this book, the invitation is simple: experiment. Notice the connections within and beyond your team. Pay attention to the conversations you are not yet having. Commit to learning together. In doing so, you create not just performance, but sustainability. And when teams sustain that fizz and buzz, they move beyond survival and revival—into thrival.

David Clutterbuck
Sheffield
United Kingdom

References

Introduction

Clutterbuck, D. (2019). *Coaching the team at work 2: The definitive guide to team coaching.* Nicholas Brealey.

Hawkins, P. (2017). *Leadership team coaching: Developing collective transformational leadership* (3rd ed.). Kogan Page.

Qualtrics. (2025, May 9). The 5 Employee Experience Trends Redefining Work in 2025. https://www.qualtrics.com/blog/employee-experience-trends/

Edmondson, A. (1999). Psychological safety and learning behavior in work teams. *Administrative Science Quarterly*, 44(2), 350–383. https://doi.org/10.2307/2666999

Gallup. (2024). State of the Global Workplace Report. https://www.gallup.com/workplace/349484/state-of-the-global-workplace.aspx

Gallup, Inc. (2024). *Gallup 2024 Q12® meta-analysis* [Report]. Gallup.

Gallup. (2025). *State of the Global Workplace Report 2025*. Gallup, Inc.

Gallup. (2025, April 18). Global indicator: Employee engagement. https://www.gallup.com/394373/indicator-employee-engagement.aspx

McKinsey & Company. (2024). *The health of high-performing teams: What drives performance in a changing world?* McKinsey Global Institute. https://www.mckinsey.com/business-functions/organization/our-insights/the-health-of-high-performing-teams

Gray, C. (Host). (2024–). *Thriving Leaders Podcast* [Audio podcast]. Spotify. https://open.spotify.com/show/59stvSfoIi7Mkavj3dOjYk?si=7713821e43dd4910

Chapter 1 – Thriving Teams

Gray, C. (Host). (2025, May 22). *Coaching the system with David Clutterbuck* [Audio podcast episode]. Thriving Culture. *Thriving Leaders Podcast*. Spotify. https://open.spotify.com/episode/0mfaqjDhuAtdOFP9D9WDhb

Katzenbach, J. R., & Smith, D. K. (1994). *The wisdom of teams: Creating the high-performance organization*. Harvard Business Review Press.

Edmondson, A. C. (1999). Psychological safety and learning behavior in work teams. *Administrative Science Quarterly*, 44(2), 350–383.

Blenko, M. W., Mankins, M. C., & Rogers, P. (2010). *Decide & Deliver: 5 Steps to Breakthrough Performance in Your Organization*. Harvard Business Press.

AWS Executive Insights. (2025, July 18). Amazon's Two Pizza Teams. https://aws.amazon.com/executive-insights/content/amazon-two-pizza-team/

Bryar, C., & Carr, B. (2021). *Working Backwards: Insights, Stories, and Secrets from Inside Amazon*. St. Martin's Press.

Hackman, J. R. (2002). *Leading Teams: Setting the Stage for Great Performances*. Boston, MA: Harvard Business School Press.

O'Malley, E., & McBride, J. F. (2023). *When Everyone Leads: The Toughest Challenges Get Seen and Solved*. Bard Press.

Heifetz, R. A., Linsky, M., & Grashow, A. (2009). *The Practice of Adaptive Leadership: Tools and Tactics for Changing Your Organization and the World*. Harvard Business Press.

Part 1 – Purpose

Frankl, V. E. (1959/2006). *Man's Search for Meaning*. Boston, MA: Beacon Press.

Chapter 2 – Team Purpose

Mankins, M. C. (2004). Stop wasting valuable time. *Harvard Business Review*, 82(9), 58–65. https://hbr.org/2004/09/stop-wasting-valuable-time

Sinek, S. (2009, September). *How great leaders inspire action* [TED Talk]. TEDxPuget Sound.

Peterson, C., & Seligman, M. E. P. (2004). *Character Strengths and Virtues: A Handbook and Classification*. Oxford University Press and American Psychological Association.

VIA Institute on Character. (n.d.). The Science of Character. https://www.viacharacter.org/research

Chapter 3 – Meaningful Work

Pink, D. H. (2009). *Drive: The Surprising Truth About What Motivates Us*. Riverhead Books.

McKinsey & Company. (2021, June 28). Making work meaningful from the C-suite to the frontline. https://www.mckinsey.com/capabilities/people-and-organizational-performance/our-insights/the-organization-blog/making-work-meaningful-from-the-c-suite-to-the-frontline

KPMG. (2014). Purpose in Focus: KPMG Survey. https://assets.kpmg.com/content/dam/kpmg/xx/pdf/2019/10/global-customer-experience-excellence-report.pdf

Joly, H. (2021). *The Heart of Business: Leadership Principles for the Next Era of Capitalism*. Harvard Business Review Press.

Mogi, K. (2017). *The Little Book of Ikigai: The Essential Japanese Way to Finding Your Purpose in Life*. Quercus Editions.

Beaumont People. (2023). *Meaningful Work Insights Report 2023*. Beaumont People.

Gallup. (2024). State of the Global Workplace Report. https://www.gallup.com/workplace/349484/state-of-the-global-workplace.aspx

Collins, J. (2001). Good to Great: *Why Some Companies Make the Leap... and Others Don't*. HarperBusiness.

Bartlett, S. (Host). (2021–2025). The Diary of a CEO. https://www.youtube.com/@TheDiaryOfACEO

Part 2 – Relationships

Waldinger, R., & Schulz, M. (2023). *The good life: Lessons from the world's longest scientific study of happiness*. Simon & Schuster.

Gallup. (2024). Gallup Q12 Meta-Analysis Report: The relationship between employee engagement and organizational outcomes. Gallup, Inc. https://www.gallup.com/workplace/321725/gallup-q12-meta-analysis-report.aspx

Gray, C. (Host). (2024, April 18). *Strengths, engagement & work besties with Claire DeCarteret* [Audio podcast episode]. In *Thriving Leaders Podcast*. Spotify. https://open.spotify.comepisode/6M1EUJdWH8So0NgvVuMNBd?si=mgZmrDgcTbyBGy4b6xqWyw

Gray, C. (Host). (2025, July 24). Kindness, accountability and trust at Insync with Jeremy Summers [Audio podcast episode]. *Thriving Leaders Podcast.* Spotify. https://open.spotify.com/episode/5eIBOsXgLbNe8STNkjmNDp?si=ljiMIod5Tr-n4MMkInK1_Q

Chapter 4 – Psychological Safety

Gray, C. (Host). (2025, March 26). Learning teams: Psychological safety, accountability, and failure with Amy Edmondson [Audio podcast episode]. *Thriving Leaders Podcast.* Spotify. https://open.spotify.com/episode/1W9gV9aPOAnTWWiiRPCPJF?si=XPpK-2zkSpWt4bYnjOJzkg

Edmondson, A. C. (1999). Psychological Safety and Learning Behavior in Work Teams. *Administrative Science Quarterly*, 44(4), 350–383.

Duhigg, C. (2016, February 25). What Google learned from its quest to build the perfect team. *The New York Times Magazine.*

Koopmann, J., Lanaj, K., Wang, M., Zhou, L., & Shi, J. (2016). Nonlinear effects of team tenure on team psychological safety climate and climate strength: Implications for average team member performance. *Journal of Applied Psychology*, 101(7), 940–957. https://doi.org/10.1037/apl0000121

McKinsey & Company. (2021, July). Psychological safety and the critical role of leadership development. https://www.mckinsey.com/capabilities/people-and-organizational-performance/our-insights/psychological-safety-and-the-critical-role-of-leadership-development

In 't Anker, M. S. (2023). *Observed psychological safety and individual job performance: Behavioral differences in monocultural and multicultural agile teams* (Bachelor's thesis, University of Twente). University of Twente Student Theses. https://purl.utwente.nl/essays/95339

Hofstede Insights. (n.d.). Country comparison: Australia. Hofstede Insights. https://www.hofstede-insights.com/country-comparison/australia/

UK Essays. (2014). Hofstede's cultural dimensions in Australia. https://www.ukessays.com/essays/cultural-studies/key-dimensions-of-national-culture-in-pakistan-cultural-studies-essay.php?vref=1

Deakin University study of 265 Australian workers (cited in *HBR Leading Global Teams Effectively*)

Rider, C. et al. (2023, March 27). Proven Tactics for Improving Teams' Psychological Safety. MIT Sloan Management Review. https://sloanreview.mit.edu/article/proven-tactics-for-improving-teams-psychological-safety/

Gray, C. (Host). (2025). From resistance to results: How Greg Pickering from AFCA turned team performance [Audio podcast episode]. In *Thriving Leaders Podcast*. Spotify. https://open.spotify.com/episode/2Cq5k2uSNlQUA0NAfjQKCy?si=TofsmxgBSKqguSMBi8fKvg

Blanding, M. (2024, July 18). New hires lose psychological safety after year one: How to fix it. Harvard Business School Working Knowledge. https://www.library.hbs.edu/working-knowledge/new-hires-lose-psychological-safety-after-year-one-how-to-fix-it

EcSell Institute. (2022). Psychological Safety: Does It Matter in the Workplace? https://ecsellinstitute.com/psych-safety-education-1/

McKinsey & Company. (2021, Feb 11). Psychological safety and the critical role of leadership development. https://www.mckinsey.com/capabilities/people-and-organizational-performance/our-insights/psychological-safety-and-the-critical-role-of-leadership-development

Clarke, T. R. (2020). *The 4 Stages of Psychological Safety: Defining the Path to Inclusion and Innovation*. Berrett-Koehler.

Chapter 5 – Trust

Ross, S. (2024, May 17). *The neurobiology of trust and its impact on team performance*. Sana Ross blog.

McKinsey & Company. (2024). *The State of Trust in Organizations Report*.

Lencioni, P. (2002). *The Five Dysfunctions of a Team: A Leadership Fable*. Jossey-Bass.

Covey, S. R. (1989). *The 7 habits of highly effective people*. Free Press.

Gottman, J. M. (1994). *Why marriages succeed or fail: And how you can make yours last*. Simon & Schuster.

Reina, D. S., & Reina, M. L. (2023). *Trust and betrayal in the workplace: Building effective relationships in your organization* (3rd ed.). Berrett-Koehler Publishers.

Covey, S. M. R. (2006). *The Speed of Trust: The One Thing That Changes Everything*. Free Press.

Botsman, R. (2020). *How to Trust and Be Trusted*. TED, Ideas Worth Spreading. https://ideas.ted.com/how-to-trust-and-be-trusted/

BetterUp. (2019). The Value of Belonging at Work: New Research on the Business and Personal Impact of Belonging. https://www.betterup.com/

Gray, C. (Host). (2025). From resistance to results: How Greg Pickering from AFCA turned team performance [Audio podcast episode]. In *Thriving Leaders Podcast*. Spotify. https://open.spotify.com/episode/2Cq5k2uSNlQUA0NAfjQKCy?si=TofsmxgBSKqguSMBi8fKvg

Chapter 6 – Clear Direction

Inayatullah, S. (2013). *Futures Studies: Theories and Methods*. World Futures Studies Federation.

Velasquez, G., & Starrk, E. (2023, September 8). When You're Asked to Meet Impossible Goals. *Harvard Business Review*.

Sinek, S. (2019). *The infinite game*. Portfolio/Penguin.

Gray, C. (Host). (2025, August 7). Olympic-Level Leadership Lessons with Matt Carroll [Audio podcast episode]. *Thriving Leaders Podcast*. Spotify. https://open.spotify.com/episode/7rjpwwnEgbfKQ6uYXrGc0b?si=YDhcAn8eTyqygP1bbpkW0Q

Chapter 7 – Team Accountability

Culture Partners. (2024). Landmark Workplace Study Reveals Crisis of Accountability. https://culturepartners.com/insights/landmark-workplace-study-reveals-crisis-of-accountability/

Gallup. (2025). *State of the Global Workplace Report*. https://www.gallup.com/workplace/349484/state-of-the-global-workplace.aspx

Carucci, R. (2020, November 23). How to Actually Encourage Employee Accountability. *Harvard Business Review*.

Google re: Work (2016). Guide: Understand team effectiveness. https://rework.withgoogle.com/print/guides/5721312655835136/

American Society for Training and Development (ASTD), now Association for Talent Development (ATD), reported statistics circa 2010 on goal commitment and accountability.

Part 4 – Connection

Friedman, R. (2021). 5 Things High-Performing Teams Do Differently. *Harvard Business Review*. https://hbr.org/2021/10/5-things-high-performing-teams-do-differently

Chapter 8 – Togetherness

Gallup. (2025, May 2). Neurodiverse Workers: Hidden Challenges, Untapped Potential. https://www.gallup.com/workplace/659618/neurodiverse-workers-hidden-challenges-untapped-potential.aspx

Katzenbach, J. R., & Smith, D. K. (1993). *The wisdom of teams: Creating the high-performance organization.* Harvard Business Review Press.

Chapter 9 – Team Processes

Microsoft Work Trend Index. (2023). Annual Report.

Venkatesh Babu, T. S., & Venkatesan, G. (2023). *Analyzing The Organization's Team Dynamics And Employees Performance Affected By The Emergence Of Remote Work.*

McKinsey & Company. (2024). The future of the office. https://www.mckinsey.com/industries/real-estate/our-insights/the-future-of-the-office

Cappelli, P., & Nehmeh, R. (2025). Hybrid Still Isn't Working. *Harvard Business Review*, July–August 2025. https://hbr.org/2025/07/hybrid-still-isnt-working

Flowtrace. (2025). *State of Meetings Report.* https://www.flowtrace.co/collaboration-blog/state-of-meetings-report

Duhigg, C. (2021, October). 5 things high-performing teams do differently. *Harvard Business Review.* Retrieved August 4, 2025, from https://hbr.org/2021/10/5-things-high-performing-teams-do-differently

Slack. (n.d.). Case study: What happened when we took a break at Slack. Slack Blog. Retrieved August 4, 2025, from https://slack.com/intl/en-au/blog/productivity/case-study-what-happened-when-we-took-a-break-at-slack

Hadley, C. N., Zakhour, M., Mahfouz, M., & Cosmic Centaurs. (2025). The Surprising Power of Team Rituals. *Harvard Business Review*. https://hbr.org/2025/01/the-surprising-power-of-team-rituals

Gilkey, C. (2023). *Team Habits: How Small Actions Lead to Extraordinary Results*. Hachette Go.

Cisco Global Hybrid Work Study 2025: https://gadget.co.za/ciscohybridwork78t/ | https://newsroom.cisco.com/c/dam/r/newsroom/pdfs/Cisco-Hybrid-Work-Study.pdf

Atlassian. (2025). *State of Teams: Collaboration and Productivity Report*. Atlassian. https://www.atlassian.com/blog/state-of-teams-2025

Right to Disconnect (AU law): https://www.fairwork.gov.au/employment-conditions/hours-of-work-breaks-and-rosters/right-to-disconnect | https://www.bbc.com/news/articles/c5y32g7203vo

PwC Australia: https://www.pwc.com.au/workforce/people-and-organisation-matters/the-future-of-work-is-hybrid-but-how-do-you-make-it-a-success.html

McKinsey & Company. (2024). The Future of the Office. https://www.mckinsey.com/industries/real-estate/our-insights/the-future-of-the-office

Gray, C. (Host). (2025, April 10). From busy to effective: Mastering team productivity with Dermot Crowley [Audio podcast episode]. *Thriving Leaders Podcast*. Spotify. https://open.spotify.com/episode/3xMjBjbf3eQ5E8QZFWBVOx?si=s-myZ3naRZeQmpXm0OnBeg

Covey, S. R. (1989). *The 7 Habits of Highly Effective People*. Free Press.

Rock, D. (2009). *Your Brain at Work: Strategies for Overcoming Distraction, Regaining Focus, and Working Smarter All Day Long*. HarperBusiness.

Gray, C. (Host). (2025, August 20). AI and Large Language Model's (LLMs) in Thriving Teams [Audio podcast episode]. *Thriving Leaders Podcast*. Spotify. https://open.spotify.com/episode/7lhPTnlFoIhzKI2VlduhW0?si=0fs2rrGASWmnAiWDlUzfXw

Crowley, D. (2020). *Smart teams: How to work better together*. Wiley.

Part 5 – Challenge and Support

Edmondson, A. C. (2019). *The fearless organization: Creating psychological safety in the workplace for learning, innovation, and growth.* Wiley.

McKinsey & Company. (2021). Psychological safety and the critical role of leadership development. https://www.mckinsey.com/capabilities/people-and-organizational-performance/our-insights/psychological-safety-and-the-critical-role-of-leadership-development

Chapter 10 – Healthy Debate

Cinardo, J. (2011). Gender dynamics and conflict at work. In J. Cinardo (Ed.), *Workplace conflict: Gender and negotiation.* Routledge.

Meyer, E. (2014). *The culture map: Breaking through the invisible boundaries of global business.* PublicAffairs.

Livermore, D. (2025). *Leading with Cultural Intelligence* (3rd ed.). AMACOM.

NASA. (1986). *Report of the Presidential Commission on the Space Shuttle Challenger Accident.*

NASA. (2003). *Columbia Accident Investigation Board Report.*

Brownell, J. (2012). *Listening: Attitudes, principles, and skills* (5th ed.). Pearson.

Rock, D. (2008). SCARF: A brain-based model for collaborating with and influencing others. *NeuroLeadership Journal,* (1), 1–9. https://doi.org/10.2139/ssrn.1901535

Heifetz, R. A., Grashow, A., & Linsky, M. (2009). *The practice of adaptive leadership: Tools and tactics for changing your organization and the world.* Harvard Business Press.

Nichols, R. G., & Stevens, L. A. (1957). *Are you listening?* McGraw-Hill.

Wetzler, T. (2025). *The Curiosity Curve: Transforming Conversations Through Mindset.* Beacon Press.

Whitmore, J. (2017). *Coaching for Performance* (5th ed.). Nicholas Brealey Publishing.

Grant, A. (2021). *Think again: The power of knowing what you don't know.* Viking.

Marcus, L. J., Dorn, B. C., & Henderson, J. M. (2019). *You're It: Crisis, Change, and How to Lead When It Matters Most.* PublicAffairs.

de Bono, E. (1985). *Six Thinking Hats*. Little, Brown & Company.

Guilford, J. P. (1956). The structure of intellect. *Psychological Bulletin*, 53(4), 267–293.

Kahneman, D. (2011). *Thinking, fast and slow*. Farrar, Straus and Giroux.

Snowden, D. J., & Boone, M. E. (2007). A leader's framework for decision making. *Harvard Business Review*, 85(11), 68–76.

Argyris, C. (1990). *Overcoming organizational defenses: Facilitating organizational learning*. Allyn & Bacon.

Chapter 11 – Learning

Edmondson, A. C. (2019). *The fearless organization: Creating psychological safety in the workplace for learning, innovation, and growth*. Wiley.

Edmondson, A. C. (2023). *Right kind of wrong: The science of failing well*. Atria Books.

Harvard Business Review. (2025). The Rhythm of Team Learning: How High-Performing Innovation Teams Structure Their Growth. *Harvard Business Review*, July/August 2025.

Dweck, C. S. (2006). *Mindset: The new psychology of success*. Random House.

Dyer, W.G. Jr. & Dyer, J.H. (2023). *Team Building: Proven Strategies for Improving Team Performance*.

Gray, C. (Host). (2025, June 26). Peernovation: Unlocking team potential with Leo Bottary [Audio podcast episode]. *Thriving Leaders Podcast*. Spotify. https://open.spotify.com/episode/7wwipvHxoctrnETy3lpXD0?si=p5WsWdyKQxW957Xg4Y-xLA

Part 6 – Alignment

Deloitte. (2025). *2025 Global Human Capital Trends: The Great Reimagination. Deloitte Insights*. https://www2.deloitte.com/

Chapter 12 – Team alignment

McKinsey & Company. (2023). The State of Organizations 2023: Ten shifts transforming organizations. https://www.mckinsey.com/capabilities/people-and-organizational-performance/our-insights/the-state-of-organizations-2023

De Smet, A., D'Auria, G., Meijknecht, L., & Albaharna, M. (2024, October 31). Go, teams: When teams get healthier, the whole organization benefits. McKinsey & Company. https://www.mckinsey.com/capabilities/people-and-organizational-performance/our-insights/go-teams-when-teams-get-healthier-the-whole-organization-benefits

Schultz, W. (2016). Dopamine reward prediction-error signalling: A two-component response. *Nature Reviews Neuroscience*, 17(3), 183–195. https://doi.org/10.1038/nrn.2015.26

Thompson, G. (2025). *Collaborative Brain: Neuroscience at Work*. Stanford University Press.

Zak, P. (2017). The neuroscience of trust. *Harvard Business Review*. Viewer's oxytocin insights linking trust with performance.

Chapter 13 – Stakeholder alignment

Johnson, B. (1996, 2020). *Polarity management: Identifying and managing unsolvable problems* (2nd ed.). HRD Press.

Gray, C. (Host). (2025, June 5). When everyone leads: A deep dive into adaptive leadership with Kaye Monk-Morgan [Audio podcast episode]. *Thriving Leaders Podcast*. Spotify. https://open.spotify.com/episode/18gkXqPljd3TARTi8I5aTU?si=Vg5a1 5xHSKC5UUk5WpVlOw

Mendelow, A. L. (1991). *Environmental scanning: The impact of the stakeholder concept*. ICIS 1991 Proceedings.

Gardner, H. K. (2017). *Smart Collaboration: How Professionals and Their Firms Succeed by Breaking Down Silos*. Harvard Business Review Press.

Gardner, H. K., & Matviak, I. (2022). *Smarter Collaboration: A New Approach to Breaking Down Barriers and Transforming Work*. Harvard Business Review Press.

Bahr, N., & Chamberlain, K. (2024). Collaborating is taking too much of our time. *Harvard Business Review*. Retrieved from https://hbr.org/2024/01/collaborating-is-taking-too-much-of-our-time

Kahane, A. (2017). *Collaborating with the enemy: How to work with people you don't agree with or like or trust*. Berrett-Koehler Publishers.

Gartner. (2024). *Collaboration Drag: Managing the Dark Side of Teamwork*. Gartner Research Note.